THE
ANGEL
EXPERIENCE

ALSO BY TERRY LYNN TAYLOR

Messengers of Light: The Angels' Guide to Spiritual Growth

Guardians of Hope: The Angels' Guide to Personal Growth

Answers from the Angels: A Book of Angel Letters

Creating with the Angels, An Angel-Guided Journey into Creativity

Angel Wisdom: 365 Meditations and Insights from the Heavens
(co-author, Mary Beth Crain)

Angel Days: A Journal and Daybook for Everyone
Who Walks with Angels

The Alchemy of Prayer, Rekindling Our Inner Life

The Optimystic's Handbook: Using Mystical Wisdom to Discover
Hope, Happiness, and the Wonder of Spiritual Living
(co-author, Mary Beth Crain)

THE
ANGEL
EXPERIENCE

Simple Ways to Cultivate
the Qualities of the Divine

TERRY LYNN
TAYLOR

AMBER-ALLEN PUBLISHING

SAN RAFAEL, CALIFORNIA

Published by Amber-Allen Publishing, Inc.
Post Office Box 6657
San Rafael, California 94903

Editorial: Nancy Carleton
Cover and Text Design: Nita Ybarra Design
Angel Photo: © John Weber, Graphistock, New York
Author Photo: Catherine Ledner
Typography: Rick Gordon, Emerald Valley Graphics

Library of Congress Cataloging-in-Publication Data

Taylor, Terry Lynn, 1955–
    The angel experience : simple ways to cultivate the
qualities of the divine / by Terry Lynn Taylor. p. cm.
        ISBN 1-878424-35-1 (alk. paper)
    1. Angels–Miscellanea. 2. Spiritual life. I. Title.
            BL477.T37 1998
            291.2′15–dc21
            98-20693   CIP

Printed in Canada on acid-free paper
Distributed by Publishers Group West
10 9 8 7 6 5 4 3 2 1

To me, life is about creating beautiful stories from our deepest experiences. In this book, you will find several stories about my friend Jai, who responds to life with courage and an open heart, and serves "on call for the angels of God." This book is for Jai, with gratitude for her being a mentor in feminine wisdom, an angel on call, and most important, a true soul-sister friend.

—T. L. T.

Contents

CONTENTS

THE
ANGEL
EXPERIENCE

ANGELS: THE TIMELESS
CONSCIOUSNESS OF LOVE

O NE DAY WHILE READING, I came across the G. K. Chesterton saying "Angels can fly because they take themselves lightly." This little saying hit my consciousness like a blast of light, and the entire room seemed to grow lighter. I stopped reading and stayed with this exciting feeling. Two important insights came to me in that moment. One, I was taking my life far too seriously, and not respecting the lighter, humorous side of God. Two, I was forgetting that the angels are our spiritual helpers and guides in life.

I had always believed in angels, and had experienced angelic intervention in times of crisis, but in that moment I experienced an expanded idea of what the angels represent. Along with a deeper appreciation for divine humor came a renewed appreciation for life on Earth and the importance of our humanity. Ironically, the angels, who could be thought of as pure spirit, helped me to honor the significance of being human.

Ever since that day, the idea of an angel experience has been ever-present. By "angel experience" I mean the qualities of consciousness that allow us to feel a deeper connection with the angels, and a deeper experience of what it means to be human. People love to hear about angel experiences that others have had, and they love to share their own, however, this book is not a collection of angel stories. I may refer to a story here and there, but the focus is not on exploring the existence of angels, because I take this as a given. I am interested in what the angels want us to know, and in how they guide us to embrace life more fully. I want to strengthen our relationship with the angels by sharing simple ways we can make angel consciousness a vital part of our everyday lives.

The angels help us understand the importance of our physical human experience. The angels remind us that we are called to love, and that we each have a unique way to express love. By working and playing with the angels, we naturally experience as much love as we dare to while we are here on Earth. Profound life transformations and changes of heart take place after an experience of divine love by way of an angel. People who have experienced real transformations of consciousness with the angels receive heavenly grace, blessings, and hope in their darkest hours. A divine sense of humor makes their lives soar with love, light, and laughter.

When the angels touch our hearts and "kiss our minds," we are forever changed. Our wonder in being human comes back strong with angelic guidance. The magic of nature, the mythic quality of being human, the pain of the soul, the soaring of the spirit, the beauty of compassion, and the grace of reverence all come together, weaving life into a meaningful experience.

⤜✦⟤⟢✦⤛

Can the angels help lead us to true happiness?
Can we ask the angels for help on the practical matters of living?
What are the angels doing right now?
What goes on in Heaven that we need to be mindful of?
How can we feel more at home with being human?

These are some of the questions that led me to write *Messengers of Light,* which was published in the spring of 1990. Since then, I have written eight books to help people with their growing consciousness of angels. The books I wrote came to be called "angel books," and I became part of a publishing boom that propelled the popularity of angels. As I write this book, people talk about the recent interest in angels as a fad now rendered passé. I have heard people say that they are "burnt out" on all things related to angels.

The angels are not a song to get tired of hearing, or a fad we can replace with another new fad. Fads come and go, but what is genuine can never be destroyed. The genuine will always reemerge fully intact, while the unreal, phony, and fraudulent will pass away over time. The angels have been around since the beginning of time, and they are always there, waiting for the right moment to touch our lives.

My main goal will always be to keep the message of the angels alive. I don't want their beautiful message of hope and love to get lost because a publishing trend is over. The reasons for the angels' presence in our lives have not disappeared; angels continue to play a huge role in many people's lives and their message is more important than ever. Numerous people continue to write me letters sharing how the angels have blessed their lives; their connection with the angels has grown stronger, not weaker. I have heard so many rich stories of everyday people who have experienced a transformation of their hearts when the angels touched their lives and brought them closer to God.

I recently visited a traveling art exhibit entitled "The Invisible Made Visible: Angels from the Vatican." It was crowded, and people were excited to be in a room with these awe-inspiring images. I believe that a new and deeper angelic wave of inspiration is coming. The angels are bringing us a new consciousness, one that we can mature with gracefully. This consciousness will allow us to live in peace amid the chaos of our times.

We all hear about how bad the world is, how stressful life has become, and how crazy everything seems to be. I feel this way often, but only for fleeting moments. Life is not always easy; our saving grace is to be flexible — to open our hearts and trust in divine love even when we feel cast away from it. If we examine our lives truthfully, there are also beautiful experiences and blessed moments. We see that life is great quite often, that people who are good at heart are all around us, and that the tough parts, in time, become a simple matter of changing our perception.

The material in this book is organized into short chapters, each intended to cultivate an experience of the divine in our lives. The topics I have chosen are inspired by real struggles people have shared with me in their quest to evolve with the angels. Even though the word *angel* doesn't appear in every sentence, the angels are in the space surrounding every page. I encourage you to continue living with the angels so that they can bring you a stronger spiritual connection to life. Think of the angels as you read this book, and they will inspire you to remember that you are loved in Heaven with a love that can heal the deepest wound, create the most unimaginable miracle, and bring you grace in the darkest moments of pain.

Our true human nature is divine and our relationship with the angels is one of give-and-take. The angels respond to our divinity, and they want us to respond to the inspiration they send us. We are called to help the angels, and the angels are called to help us. Angel experiences come from those times when you risk little fears to love deeply. Great experiences come from taking chances — not sitting back and wondering what it would be like to do something, but getting out there and doing it.

I am often asked about my latest angel experience. I always answer: It is happening right now. *Now* is your angel experience too, and the more you recognize the presence of angels, the more frequent and inspiring your angel experiences will be.

As an Angel

To study angels is to shed light on ourselves,
especially those aspects of ourselves that have been
put down in our secularized civilization, our secularized
educational systems, and even our secularized
worship system. By secularization, I mean
anything that sucks the awe out of things.
—MATTHEW FOX, *The Physics of Angels*

IMAGINE FOR A MOMENT that you are an angel assigned to watch over humans. You are a being of pure light and spirit; you can be wherever you need to be in an instant. You do all you do for the Great Creator of Love, with divine beauty, grace, and enlightenment. You have spent eternity watching humans. You have seen all the missed opportunities for love, and watched humans blessed with all they need to bring them delight and happiness continually suffer through life. You have witnessed and helped create profound moments that allow humans to become truly inspired. You have seen hearts open in these profound moments, when love is imprinted on the world in ways that exceed the reach of human imagination.

As an angel you may find yourself curious about the way humans can physically create love, beauty, and life itself. A human can reach out and hug a loved one in a warm exchange of sweetness. Humans can be physically present for one another in moments of compassion in which great healing takes place. This is something you have witnessed and facilitated many times as an angel, but you have never been able to experience the physical connection itself.

You have witnessed the joy that humans feel who make love the reason of their lives, so you take a leap of faith and ask God to be born as a human. As an angel now human, you are ready to create the physical expression of love. You want to fully explore the physical elements of Earthly existence: the warmth of a fire, the soothing feel of water, the magic of air, and the comfort of trees. All of these sensations naturally fill you with a sense of awe and delight.

As an angel now human, you experience the full range of human emotions; you feel the pain of loss; you miss loved ones when they go away. Human life teaches you the ways in which humans fear that they are not good enough and not doing enough, and how they kick and torment themselves when opportunities pass them by. Eventually you begin to understand the fatigue that life can bring. Sometimes you fail to live up to your ideals and you now understand what it is like to pursue a dream and get lost along the way.

As an angel now human, you share in all the absurd ways humans miss the simple beauty in life. Many times as an angel you tried to attract a person's attention to get them to stop and take note of a beautiful sunset they were ignoring. Humans so often forget to look up and witness a beautiful cloud painting the angels have done just for them. Angels note the day when the childlike wonder of humans is replaced by worries and stress.

Humans have so many choices and possibilities, but sometimes they forget that they don't have to sit around and cry about a tragedy when the sun is out. Humans always have the choice to go out and play, and to have a good laugh while playing. There are no rules concerning how humans deal with sadness and grief, or how much joy their hearts can hold.

As an angel now human, dealing with material worth and the concept of money prove particularly difficult, because money is so arbitrary, yet so central to being human. As an angel, you have watched humans chase after money, better jobs, and more fulfilling relationships. You have also wondered why humans would insult God by thinking that the key to happiness lies in attaining a more perfect physical appearance. Physical imperfections are unique reflections of the holy spirit. You cannot understand why more people don't enjoy getting old and keeping childlike wonder alive.

You have watched humans choose security and boredom over new experiences that would delight and enrich them. In a human's obsession with time, they forget that this very moment is one of the most glorious opportunities God has ever bestowed on them. There are so many simple things humans could do to make life a heavenly experience from the perspective of an angel.

From this brief reflection on human life from an angel's perspective, we may wonder if it's best for the angels to stay where they have their beautiful perspective of the gift of human life, holding the vision for us and encouraging us to find ways to enjoy our time while we are here. For our part, we must reach a place where we can receive the inspiration the angels send our way. When we establish a sacred place within us where we meet the angels, we can allow ourselves to see with new eyes; we can open our heart to divine love, all the while honoring what it truly means to be human.

Have you ever wanted to be like the angels, or imagined yourself as an angel? Remember that the angels spend all their time praising and loving God. If we were to do this in our lives, we would indeed be living as the angels do.

. . . .

PRACTICE IDEA: *Wonder and Awe*

Pretend that you are an angel who just recently entered your body. Start in the morning, and be amazed at what you find in your kitchen. If you are like me, you first venture into the kitchen to make a cup of coffee. Remember, this is your very first morning. Go in, and take the lid off your jar of coffee beans. Take a good look at them. What a wonder, what a rich brown color! Then grind the beans and enjoy the fullness of their aroma. Watch the water as it catches the sunlight on its way into the pot. As your coffee brews, think about all the amazing things you can create in your own kitchen.

Now stop for a moment and listen to the birds singing. Then walk out your door and facing east, take in a deep breath of fresh morning air. Be grateful for everything you encounter. When it is time to take a shower, thank the water for cleansing away the dross of the previous day.

Allow the action of washing your hair to become a mystical experience as you slowly transfer the shampoo from the bottle to your hair, marveling in its fragrance and ability to turn into lather. Because all of these experiences are new to you, *pay attention,* so that you will learn and appreciate being physically alive.

Use your imagination and approach being an angel the best way you personally know how. There is no way to fail — there is only the joy of exploration. There is no right or wrong, no good way or bad way; there is just your way. With the angels' divine guidance, you will know how to live at your very best. Play with this perception anytime you want, especially if you feel you have gotten out of step with life. Whenever you get caught up in the fast pace of worldly life, let the angels remind you of the wonder and awe of being alive.

· 2 ·

ANGELS WATCHING
OVER US

As above, so below;
as below, so above.

—HERMES TRISMEGISTUS

T HE ANGELS WATCH OVER us and are with us all the
time. They witness all we do; yet they do not judge us
as good or bad. Angels do not decide whether we are worthy of their blessings; God has already decided that. In the
eyes of the Divine, we are beyond worth. We are valuable
because of our noble birth as humans. The problem is that
we don't always behave nobly born, so we are not always
treated this way by ourselves and the world. But we can learn
from our mistakes; we can solve this problem so that our life
becomes a divine experience in which our whole being is
an offering to the divinity of life, for the highest good of all.

Angels do not judge us; they respond to us. They respond and interact with us based on the quality of our frequency. Particular vibrations are created from our behavior and our intentions. The angels only encourage certain modes of consciousness and qualities in our behavior. The angels cannot help us with greed-based goals; they can only help us with our higher purpose.

If your motivation to be spiritual includes the desire to master the material world — "to have it all" — you will find that the angels aren't interested in conspicuous consumption. While they rejoice when you enjoy the rewards of physical existence, they are most interested in helping you *want what you have* in a creative, blessed way. This doesn't mean you cannot have prosperity and abundance with angel consciousness — quite the contrary. But there is a fine line between enjoying material prosperity and giving into greed, and it has to do with motivation.

When we choose to work and play with the angels, we need to explore the issue of motivation. Working with the angels is a matter of attuning our vibration and building our soul with human virtues. This means our motivations need to be in alignment with what the angels respond to. If you are motivated to know angels so that you can escape the pain and suffering of life, you will find that the angels guide you instead toward accepting the pain and discovering the strength that is within you for facing problems with courage. Your motivation may start with a desire to escape the pain, but you can learn how to be present with pain, and have a direct experience of what it has to say to you. By awakening to angelic presence, you will be open to having a deeper experience of joy, and you will discover that joy is often born from pain.

It is not an angel's job to punish or to "right the wrongs" of human behavior. When we feel we are being punished, we have to realize that we are the interpreters of our experience. We are the ones doing much of the judging, and often carrying out our own punishments. The angels of God hold us in love. We need to remind ourselves that love is never a means of power and control, so our relationship with the Divine is not a power struggle. To have a good relationship with the angels, we don't need to possess them, or continually seek proof of their love. All that is required is that we accept the love and allow the love to energize us with the intent to reconnect to the Source in our own special way. The angels' message calls on us to move back to the place of loving God for our sustenance.

In the last decade or so of the New Consciousness movement, millions of people have found that spiritual principles sought outside a religious context can make our lives better. We have seen our lives turn around just by turning around our own attitudes. We have discovered ways of empowering ourselves in a world that often seems upside down and difficult to navigate. Sometimes a newfound spiritual awakening coincides with material wealth and prosperity, so naturally we want more and feel that our spiritual principles will bring us everything that our hearts desire.

In order to stay centered in changing times, and for our spiritual paths to evolve, we need to cultivate the qualities of gratitude and humility. Lately, whenever I feel even the slightest bit smug, I next get a very clear lesson that humbles me and makes me look at what I was avoiding. Sometimes lessons in humility include a painful, daunting realization, and other times they come in the form of a gentler, loving nudge. The world of the angels brings us into a place of humility and gratitude. No matter what happens, by remembering these two qualities and using them as they are meant to be used, we can meet our challenges on higher ground.

. . . .

PRACTICE IDEA: *Gratitude and Humility*

Gratitude is the water you need to activate the seeds of divine qualities. Gratitude is a "great attitude" to travel with when you are seeking communion with the angels; they respond to gratitude instantly. Even if you begin with a half-hearted attempt, the angels will come in and help your whole heart to feel grateful. There is a distinction between thankfulness and gratitude. You can say the words "thank you" and then turn around and be ungrateful a moment later. The saying goes: "Our thankfulness is measured by the number of our words; our gratitude is measured by the nature of our actions."

Many people find it beneficial to keep a gratitude journal, which is like music to the angels. To start your gratitude journal, make a list of at least five things that happen each day that you can be grateful for. You might want to add to this list five things that humble you in the course of your day — not things that humiliated you, but ways you changed your perception from "you at the center" to "you as part of the whole." You don't need to think less of yourself, but think of yourself less. When you incorporate a sense of gratitude and humility each day, you will naturally activate the seeds of the divine.

GRACE HAPPENS

Behind all physical phenomena lie
specific archetypal spiritual forces . . .
impulses playing within our life through nature,
through the angels, touching us at atomic levels.
—TED ANDREWS, *Sacred Sounds*

WHEN THE ANGELS REACH us in a time of despair and infuse our consciousness with love, a shift takes place that lightens our viewpoint, and helps us realize that there is so much more to life than little human worries. When the angels bless our consciousness, a miracle occurs. Our heart begins to open like a flower with infinite petals, and we discover a new depth to life and love. This is grace.

God may bless you with grace, no matter where you are, or what the conditions of your life. But we cannot demand that grace come to us. It is the same with the angels: We can know them, but we cannot demand that they do something for us. Yet, there are things we can do to put ourselves in a position to be present for grace and for the angels. Like our experience of the angels, we each have a unique experience of grace; if we pay attention with our heart, we will recognize it. If we take the time to have reverence for the world we live in, we become blessed by it.

One of the most beautiful things about grace is that it is unearned. It does not come because we have followed a set of rules; it does not visit us because we have been good little girls and boys, and it can never be bought or controlled by human beings. Like anything beautiful, if we chase it we are only left with a sense that we have missed it. We don't need to chase after God and the angels; they are right here, and so is amazing grace. We just need to relax and raise our vibration by becoming more attuned to the qualities of Heaven, and then express our gratitude to keep the connection alive.

There is no need to explain an angel experience. Sometimes the message is in the exchange itself; it is simply a moment God and the angels have made contact with us and reminded us how loved we are in Heaven. Many people have told me about a beautiful angel moment and asked me, "What does it mean?" Well, I cannot answer what can only be found in your own heart.

And I ask, does it have to mean something other than a humble moment of love?

❧

One afternoon my friend Jai and I were driving the back roads of Ojai — a special place in California — listening to a Judy Collins tape. Just as we approached a pond nestled at the foot of a beautiful mountain range, the song "Amazing Grace" began to play. I stopped the car and turned off the motor, but kept the music playing loud. We quietly stepped out of the car and stood on a little hill by the pond. We watched with reverence as a flock of birds appeared, and hundreds of them began to fly over the pond in a ballet of beauty, moving to the music of "Amazing Grace." Time stood still. The sky, the clouds, the mountain range, and the ground we were standing on took on a heightened sense of beauty; the angels were with us.

I experienced a deep understanding and acceptance of life in that timeless moment. Everything was intrinsically good; everything in the air seemed blessed by love. Life and death became the same. I felt that I was one of the birds flying; I was the water in the pond reflecting the surrounding beauty; I was the music sending its powerful vibrations out into the ethers. Something told me that this was what the death of the body was like — a merging with the cosmic spirit of life. Nothing to fear, unless you are afraid of feeling pure love and peace.

I have been blessed with many moments of this kind of grace. It can happen anywhere and anytime the angels merge with us and share their love. I have been in groups of people who have come together to honor the angels, and we have been lifted to unimaginable heights. I have been alone, doing nothing out of the ordinary and felt this love. Grace happens sometimes when I am out and about, and I meet the eyes of a baby or a small child. These heightened moments are not to be expected or sought, because grace is not like that. It just happens. My late great friend Kip had a deep, shamanlike connection with the angels and the devas of nature. To counteract a popular bumper sticker, he had a bumper sticker made up that said, "Grace Happens."

Always remember: *Grace happens.*

. . . .

PRACTICE IDEA: *Grace and Divine Providence*

What better place to be than in a state of grace? In a state of grace we feel in tune with Divine Providence.

But grace cannot be captured and possessed; it visits us with love and then moves on, leaving us feeling blessed and gracious. The word *gracious* comes from the word *grateful,* so again gratitude comes into play in order to cultivate graciousness. To be gracious means to be naturally kind and compassionate, refined, and pleasant; these are qualities we can actively cultivate in our lives.

To encourage Divine Providence, you need to *feel* grateful, not just say that you are grateful. The angels offer a good model of graciousness; they are gracious by nature and can help us come to a point of inner peace so that our graciousness is honest and real. When you are touched by the grace of Heaven, you will be naturally grateful because there is nothing like the bliss you will experience. Begin to practice unconditional grace by means of behaving graciously without thought of what you are getting from others. When you are gracious, you are gracious for the angels, not for favor from other humans. The angels are always ready to return your graciousness with a moment of graceful bliss.

· 4 ·

Cultivating
Divine Qualities

In my view, human and divine are not opposites.
The more fully human one becomes, the more he or
she exhibits characteristics, qualities, and behaviors
suggestive of something otherworldly or divine.
All forms of dishonesty, evil, depravity, and vice
are not expressions of one's human nature,
but distortions or perversions of human nature.
—HAROLD D. JESTER

THINK ABOUT THE IDEA of human nature for a minute. What are some of the first words that come to mind? Your thoughts will likely depend on what recent experiences you have had with others as well as the programming you received over the years. As the opening quotation suggests, consider the possibility that your true human nature is divine, and that you can be more fully divine by being more fully human. This is how the angels treat us.

The angels are our co-creative partners in life. To allow their beneficial influence to touch our lives, we must develop qualities and attitudes that "angel nature" vibrates to. Cultivating divine qualities means creating positive, uplifting vibrations. It doesn't mean you go around blissfully out of touch with what is happening down here on Earth; it means that you learn to navigate and remain on course by staying in the moment and taking care of the moment, remembering to include your divinity in each decision.

Think about what qualities the angels would naturally resonate to with their high vibrational frequency. I have given countless workshops where people come together to know the angels. At some point I always ask the group what qualities they think the angels respond to. What qualities do they think we can develop in our lives that would encourage a good give-and-take relationship with the angels? The qualities that most people list include love, compassion, tolerance, flexibility, honesty, beauty, peace, humor, joy, and most important, gratitude. If you think about it, these words represent more than concepts; they represent a true vibration that allows us to experience our divinity. By cultivating positive vibrations, we champion our own guardian angel, and in turn receive many blessings.

❦

The word *cultivate,* according to the *American Heritage Dictionary,* means "To improve and prepare (land) for raising crops; to grow or tend (a plant or crop); to form and refine, as by education; and to seek the acquaintance or good will of." The word origin is the Latin *colere,* which means to inhabit, worship, develop, and be busy. For anything to be cultivated and to grow, it must be planted or seeded. Divine qualities can be cultivated. Some of these qualities seem to be universal, and some are very personal. Only you will know the qualities that truly provide a direct link to the angels for you. The experience of these qualities creates a higher vibration, a harmonic resonance the angels respond to.

Cultivating divine qualities requires a willingness to allow the angels to guide you in the practice of these qualities. If you ask God in prayer for a quality such as forgiveness, then you are called upon to pay attention to all the times and all the ways that forgiveness is required from you. If you want abundance, you cannot live with a mentality of hoarding. If you want to practice gratitude, you must take it to heart. Gratitude that comes from the heart leads to good outcomes and sends positive, constructive vibrations far and wide.

Constructive vibrations are important for all our affirmations, healing work, and work with intention. For example, using "kill energy" to "right the wrongs," and attempt to restore balance is not a skillful way of attracting angels. So often the message we hear from society calls for us to kill pain, kill enemies, kill thoughts, and kill cancer cells. Using "kill energy," such as imagining cancer cells being destroyed, may not be the best way to alter our chemistry. People studying the effects of thought and prayer on cells have found that loving energy sends a message to return to balance, whereas "kill energy" may simply upset the balance further. Balance and wholeness offer the keys to healing.

When we are looking to create a positive change, we need to look at the whole picture. Much too often in our quest for personal power, we let our egos guide the way. We don't stop to look at all the possible outcomes our actions could have on the world around us. Sincerely look at the effect of your actions. Do your actions involve competition, taking advantage of others, or a hidden agenda?

When using affirmations, prayers, and will, we do well to remember that our affirmations need to reflect a spiritual change *we* are willing to make within. Too often we look for a change in external events, which we demand with our prayers and affirmations. God has a much more interesting idea in mind for us, and it comes to us through trust and faith, and the willingness to keep changing. To receive the blessings of God, we must know how to greet them and recognize them. Sometimes, at the last minute, just when we are ready to give up, the angels work with God to bring us the highest gifts.

. . . .

PRACTICE IDEA: *Cultivating Divine Qualities*

A person who cultivates divine qualities is a person who reflects the angel experience, because that is what the angels respond to. It is really very simple. If we are brimming with anger, resentment, and hatred, where will the angels find room to dance in our consciousness? If we continually do things to repress our soul and spirit, how can the angels participate in our lives? The angels don't ever leave us, but we can make it difficult for them to interact with us. Still, the angels wait patiently for the moment when we choose to let go of the weights we have been dragging around and look to the Divine. Then they rejoice because *on our own,* we have made the choice to open our hearts.

Choose one of the divine qualities mentioned in this chapter. You might choose love, peace, gratitude, humor, joy, compassion, or any other positive, uplifting quality. Focus on that quality as your day begins. Cultivate

it and tend to it throughout the day with your full attention. At the end of the day, look back on all the gifts this
quality has brought to you directly from the angels.

· 5 ·

DISCERNING GOOD

No limits are set to the ascent of man,
and to each and every one the highest stands open.
Here it is only your personal choice that decides.

—HASIDIC SAYING

CHANCES ARE THAT AS a young child you may have
heard the admonition "If you can't say anything nice,
don't say anything at all." Why were we told this? Nowa-
days, if we want to say something that isn't nice, we are
reminded to "judge not, lest ye be judged," a Bible verse
from the book of Matthew.

We consider people "nice" when they do what we
want them to do. When they step out of line, we are likely
to question how nice they are. We teach children this concept over and over: "Oh, what a nice person to give you
that toy!" We may even take the concept of "nice" into the

realm of the angels and God: if the Divine follows our conditions and demands, the angels are nice; if not, they are mean. The truth, however, is that the angels are honest; they have no desire to be nice.

I have met many "nice" people whose effect on my life was anything but nice. Now, how did I come to this conclusion? Am I being judgmental? I guess, in a strict sense of the word, the answer is yes. The word *judge* comes from two Latin words for law and speak and basically means "one who speaks the law." Being judgmental often includes being critical and that is where we feel offended, and with good cause. There is a lot of nasty criticism in our world today, and it can injure a sensitive psyche. Words are powerful tools, and we must be careful with them. Timothy Leary once said, "Words are the fragile freight that must carry the deepest impulses in man."

Is all criticism a judgment? Are all judgments criticism? Is an observation a judgment? Is a feeling a judgment? What if you are around someone and you get a "gut feeling" something is not right; are you being judgmental? The reason I bring all of this up is that we need to learn how to discern what carries a divine vibration and what does not. A divine vibration has nothing to do with being nice. A divine vibration may be a vibration of pain, because pain is a teacher that can lead us to joy. It is up to each of us to be true to ourselves and know what gives us an experience of divine love and what does not.

To be discerning means to be insightful and perceptive. *Discern,* in literal terms, means to separate by sifting (*dis:* apart; *cernere:* sift). Discerning is a matter of noticing distinctions. To get a true reading of a situation, use more than just your mind. What message is your body sending? To what degree is your heart opening? Does your spirit feel free, or confined and beaten down? Is your body picking up a message of danger or trust? Are you being heard or manipulated? The interpretations are all up to you, but this kind of inner work can prove valuable for anyone on a spiritual path.

Recently I encountered some unsolicited counsel from someone who told me that a certain person in my life had been "keeping my vibration from ascending." Well, this phrase stuck in my mind, not because I decided it was true, but because I question the way we sometimes use spiritual concepts to criticize and judge others. Jesus socialized with a diverse group of people. He didn't run from people because they were not behaving in a "spiritual" manner, or cast them aside because they were not vibrating at his level. His acceptance of "the unholy" transformed the hearts of many. Jesus led a short but very human life; he was honest and stayed very close to God.

As far as someone else keeping my vibration from ascending, this is far too convenient an excuse. At some point we need to take responsibility for our own vibration, and realize that if we are feeling low it is not necessarily the result of present company; it is the result of our allowing ourselves to go there. Also, we need to question whether lower or higher is always neatly correlated to bad and good; sometimes we learn the most sacred lessons when we are at our lowest, when we are fully immersed in human experience.

When the angels came into my consciousness, leaving their remarkable imprint, it occurred to me that the human experience is an important thing to honor. I had tried all sorts of ways to raise my vibration, such as not eating meat and not getting tied to earthly things, but when the angels touched my heart, I had a deep realization that these things are not the means to a spiritual end. We cannot avoid the human experience just by pushing our spirit up above the fray. The problems don't go away, and the experiences we are meant to have won't go away either.

Human lives are messy and unpredictable. People often do exactly the opposite of what we believe would be good for them. But what if this is exactly what they need to do in order to evolve? Just because people evolve in different ways does not mean they are not evolving. When I talk of raising our vibrations to connect with the angels, I don't mean this as a judgment. I mean it as a behavior of reverence, of honoring the experience of our humanity, not avoiding it.

. . . .

PRACTICE IDEA: *Discernment and Non-Judgment*

Have you been infected lately with the "nice disease"? Sometimes we feel as if life is not being nice to us. Everyone we meet and each situation we encounter is measured by how "nice" it is, and nothing really measures up the way we would like. Even when something genuinely nice happens, if we are feeling burdened by our idea of an unfriendly Universe, we will look for signs to negate the good that is happening.

Consider how you relate to the world, and how you relate to others. What do you expect from life? What are you willing to accept from others? The Universe isn't nice, and it isn't mean. It just is. Practice feeling better about being you, in your body, with your guardian angel, and start to let others be what they are. Nice or mean, who cares? Let go of any judgments about being "nice." If other people appear to be dangerous, then keep your distance. Discern what is good for you and what is not. Practice letting go of expectations that are negative, then allow the positive to naturally replace them. As Chinese wisdom says, "Cease expecting and you gain all things."

6

MYSTERY AND
MIRACLES

Who is crazier? The one who hears the thunder
and says they hear God, or the one who hears God
and says they hear thunder?

—ANONYMOUS

I'VE TALKED TO MANY people in the last twelve years about angels and miracles. One theme stays in the forefront of my mind: the idea that God is in the process of doing something transformative *in our time,* on par with what was happening during biblical times, or when Christ was walking the Earth. I have heard this idea from Christian scholars who say they cannot deny that some of the experiences people are having with angels are miracles similar to the ones Jesus performed. I also hear this idea from people who are obsessed with the fact that we are nearing a millennial marker according to the Gregorian calendar system.

The new millennium is upon us. A wind of change is sweeping the world. Even the weather is cooperating. Now, of course we are going to think that our time is significant, because this is all we know. Maybe there have been miracles and wonders of this same magnitude all along. Yet, at present in Western society, something significant *is* happening. It may be that we are taking more time to contemplate matters of the spirit. We have a greater degree of comfort due to technology, which enables us to spend more time thinking.

Often humans try to come up with absolute answers for things. In the realm of miracles, this is a waste of time. How can we prove that there are more miracles now than there were one or two thousand years ago? There is no proof that life exists beyond the three dimensions we live in. There is no way to prove a miracle, because there is always someone who can "disprove" it by restructuring the truth, much the way lawyers do with facts they don't want jurors to dwell on. And there are always the proverbial snake oil salespeople, who can trick us into believing an illusion is a miracle. So it comes down to keeping our hearts open to what is miraculous. This way we will *know* a miracle and not feel we have to prove it or disprove it.

We are missing one very important issue if we insist on proof of the miracles of God. We can try to deny things of the spirit, yet they have a real effect on our psyche. No matter what our minds say, we will encounter spirit in our dreams, in our unconscious choices, and in the messages from our guardian angel. Our psyche is part of the *animus mundi,* the soul of the world. Even if you don't like the idea that we are all connected, you *will* be affected by what the collective psyche is experiencing. The point is that we experience things that are not tangible yet have a great power in influencing our lives. This is because we operate on several levels of awareness, and we have an amazing depth to our beingness that we don't always acknowledge or use in a life-affirming way.

How do we know that an angel experience, a miracle, or any message from God is truly real? What are the fruits of the experience? Were you left with a sense of peace so deep that it relaxed every cell in your body? Were the qualities of joy, laughter, love, gratitude, and beauty naturally present in your experience? Then why argue? It incenses me when a pure heartfelt experience is contaminated with explanations by some expert coming in and discussing "what really happened." We are the only ones who know the truth of our own experiences, especially our experiences of the Divine.

When I have witnessed miracles from Heaven, I experience a feeling of true humility, giving me the sense that words should not be uttered in its wake. It is also interesting to me that of all the amazing angel stories I have heard from people, some of the most awesome transformative experiences were told to me in private. In fact, this happened recently after a workshop. A young man who had been very willing to share many personal details with the group waited until after the workshop was over and then privately shared with me a near-death experience following kidney failure when he was four years old, during which Jesus appeared to him. Sometimes our experiences are so profound and sacred that it is best to guard them as we would precious jewels, and not parade them around for all to see.

Over the years the most "spiritual" people I have known rarely have a need to explain things or seek attention for "supernatural" events happening around them; they are usually too busy doing their work and play. You might enter their house and as you walk in you notice a fragrance so pure and exquisite that you ask them what incense they are burning. They may answer that there is no incense burning; it's the angels. You get no more explanation, and they are on to another matter. The angels feel comfortable around people who don't need to explain or dissect everything. Angels especially like it when people look toward God instead of projecting magical powers on them.

I was once part of a very special women's Bible study group. The teacher was truly heart-centered, and at each meeting something mystical and heart-opening would happen. One day a man appeared in the doorway of the chapel while the teacher was speaking. The sun was behind him, so he was lit up like a vision as we turned around to look at him. The interesting thing was that he was dressed in old, worn-out, dirt-stained clothes, but as he stood there in the wide doorway back-lit in sunlight, it looked like Jesus was standing there. The teacher warmly invited him in without losing the momentum of her teaching, and he quietly sat in the back. The feeling in the air was quite enlightening, and time seemed to be suspended. Here was this man whom most people would avoid if they saw on the street, but he had given us a glimpse of Jesus. He sat there for the teaching and then slipped out at some point, and no one felt the need to discuss or explain the experience; all we did was smile in our hearts and eyes.

. . . .

PRACTICE IDEA: *A Sense of Mystery*

Cultivating a sense of mystery will keep you young at heart and eternally happy. If you learn how to greet the

Mystery without demanding it to explain itself or give you a secret code to break, then you will be blessed with wonder and awe. The bottom line is that if you go seeking explanations, you will spoil many of life's experiences. The word *ex-plain* basically means to lay out flat. What if the world *were* flat and we could see everything; would this be as interesting as towering mountains and hidden valleys? I want the mysteries, the mountain with its caves and dangerous cliffs; I don't want everything explained, or left plain.

Free yourself from the explaining trap. Say, "I don't know," at least once a day. If someone asks you to explain yourself, say, "It must be the angels." Remember the words of Mary Poppins: "First of all, I would like to make one thing quite clear, I never explain anything." Try to get through one day without explaining yourself. Practice letting things mysteriously fall into place without your help.

7

AT PLAY IN THE FIELDS
OF THE PSYCHE

Every person must live the inner life in one form
or another. If we go to that realm consciously, it is by
our inner work: our prayers, meditations, dream work,
and Active Imagination. If we try to ignore the inner
world, as most of us do, the unconscious will find its way
into our lives through pathology: our psychosomatic
symptoms, compulsions, depressions, and neuroses.

—ROBERT A. JOHNSON, *Inner Work*

IN GREEK MYTHOLOGY, PSYCHE represents the personification of the soul who is loved by Eros and eventually
achieves immortality by wedding him. The classic image
of Psyche shows her with a lamp, searching for Eros. In the
myth, Psyche was not supposed to look upon Eros, but
curiosity got the better of her and she shone a light on him
while he slept. He fled, and she had to endure much hardship to be reunited with him. The myth of Psyche is said
to be an allegory for the journey of the soul, from the bliss
of preconsciousness to the pain of conscious existence, and
back to the bliss of eternal life that follows earthly death.

Another symbol of psyche as soul is symbolized by the butterfly and the metamorphosis it goes through in order to unfold its power of flight with wings of opalescent light.

In the mysterious underworld of our consciousness, on a level that is non-logical, non-linear, and non-intellectual, the angels speak to us through images, feelings, and moments of inner knowing. The psyche can only be liberated by the light of awareness that leads to love, and the angels are, first and foremost, beings of light and love. So they become our guides, leading us through the veiled mist of the "in-between world" with the lamp of awareness, toward love — love of ourselves, love of life, and love of divine truth.

We instinctively have a knowing of psyche, spirit, heart, and soul, yet we are not able to master them intellectually, because, as James Hillman notes, they are "not true concepts; rather they are symbols which evoke meanings beyond any significations we give them through definitions." Regarding definitions, it is interesting to check the *Oxford American Dictionary,* where *psyche* is defined simply as "The human soul or spirit; and the human mind." *Soul* is defined as "The spiritual or immortal element in a person; a person's mental or moral or emotional nature; a personification of a pattern; and a person, 'there's not a soul about.'"

The dictionary starts its definition of *spirit* as "A person's mind or feelings or animating principle as distinct from his body." *Spirit* has many other defining qualities listed; some are similar to the definition of soul, and yet spirit is where we diverge from the body. Spirit denotes a part of our nature that is not so strongly connected to the physical as the soul might be.

Our psychic energy is active twenty-four hours a day. When we are awake our psyche is whispering messages and images to us; and when we sleep our psyche is free to roam the infinite fields of consciousness and turn the volume up in our dreams. Psyche is usually thought of as including both the conscious and the unconscious. I like to think of our psyche as the collection of our unseen energy, a mixture of soul and spirit, with the metaphysical properties of our mind and the physical experiences of our body.

There is a message looming in the "back of our minds" asserting that we only use a small percentage of the capacity of our brain, something like 10 percent. Doesn't it seem bizarre that something so elusive could be measured and pinpointed to a number? This message haunts us with the feeling that we are not living up to our potential, that somehow we should be doing something more or something else. Well, I propose that we *are* using the rest of our brain, but we don't consciously or intellectually know it, because it is outside the realm of explanations. I also propose that there is no way we could avoid using the gray matter given to us; after all, it is living tissue. And if we become more cognizant of the full genius of our own psyche, we will experience life in a more natural way, more in synch with both our own nature and the nature of life.

When we seek to live in harmony with the unseen forces that interplay so poignantly in our lives, we find they are difficult to track and impossible to control. Understanding the intangibles, the invisibles, and our calling is done by way of our imagination. We have to be careful not to suffocate the unseen with labels, boring explanations, and answers; instead, we can unleash our imagination and learn to revere and honor the unseen daily. When seeking to understand the psyche, we have to live with many unsolved mysteries, which is good because mystery always brings a new dimension of excitement to our life. We must remember that understanding is not a destination; it is a journey of exploration.

. . . .

PRACTICE IDEA: *Know Your Selves*

When you really think about it, the oracle at Delphi should read, "Know thy *selves*," not just, "Know thyself."

We cannot escape the fact that we are multidimensional and multisensory beings. Our psyche reminds us of that mysterious feeling: we are more than our waking self in the third dimension; we have companions that are unseen. Regardless of how neatly we may organize our life, the parts of us that we ignore may start to cause us trouble. Jean Houston reminds us, "If schizophrenia is a disease of the human condition, then polyphrenia — which is the orchestration of our many selves — is health."

Start now to explore the many dimensions of who you are. Now that the angels are in your consciousness, start to know your selves. The nature of human life is like fingerpainting: we have to get our hands dirty and have some fun. Write regularly in your journal, pay attention to your dreams, and give yourself time to meditate. These are great ways to begin to connect with the deepest part of your psyche.

· 8 ·

FIGMENTS OF

OUR IMAGINATION

At an annual meeting of the American Astronomical
Association, astronomers reported the discovery of the
largest bodies ever observed in the universe. . . . Could it
be the case that these bodies of light are the Angel
breaking-through at the margins, at the breakdowns
of our systems of explanation, at the epitome of that very
way of thinking, the physics of cosmic energy levels, of
light, which initially invited the Angel to withdraw?
—ROBERT D. ROMANYSHYN, *The Angels*

I HAVE FELT AT times as if I am on a quest to remember something important. Sometimes it feels like a part of myself seems to be missing; I have vague memories of this part as if it were a dream. At other times a sense of need springs up, almost out of nowhere, and I don't know how to feed it. At these times if I look outside myself for answers or satisfaction, I feel farther away from my original quest. But when I look inside for direction by doing inner work, then I feel closer to my quest and more hopeful.

If you are interested in angels, then you know that much of your interest in and understanding of angels is an internal event, taking place in your unconscious mind. I was once told by an irate caller during a radio interview that my interest in angels was "all in my imagination." I said that I agreed, and that I knew my imagination as a place of truth, not a closed container added to my brain as an afterthought, with a limited amount of useless contents. I don't think people realize what they are saying when they use the words "It's all in your imagination" to discount an experience someone else has had, or one they have had themselves. Certainly the imagination is a tricky concept to navigate; it doesn't play by the rules, and it often brings us things we and others around us have no idea what to do with.

Often children who have never been told by their parents about angels or God start talking about God, angels, and spirit guides as if it was the most natural thing they know. The parents usually ask these children, *"Who told you that? Who has filled your head with these ideas?"* Often the answer is: "I don't know." Some parents are genuinely upset that their children would come up with "such nonsense" as angels, and other parents find a new reverence for angels and allow their children to grow up with angelic consciousness.

Very young children don't know the difference between *tell* and *show,* and they often don't understand when someone asks them how they know something. I worked in a nursery school and day care center for years, and when we wanted the children to express themselves we asked them to draw a picture, and then if they felt like it they could stand up and *show* us what they had created. Often if you use the word *tell* instead of *show,* children do not have much to say, but when they can show, then they open up and express. Even when the actual picture looks like scribbles, the child who draws it has all kinds of things to say about it. It is especially interesting when a child makes a drawing about a dream and then shares it.

When I have asked children to draw pictures of angels, they usually put wings on them and depict them watching over children doing things. When my nephew was around four years old, he drew me a picture (without me asking) of him playing T-ball, and there was an angel in the air above him, watching the game. If you ask children who draw angels whether everyone sees the angels who are watching over them, they will usually say no and yes. They know that some people do see them, and that others do not.

My point is that imagination doesn't make sense in a linear, easily explained way. Does it matter? Is it really necessary to dismiss the imagination just because the physical eyes don't take in a three-dimensional image of something? Yet, people think they are being intelligent when they ignore their imagination for something more concrete, or something that has supposedly been designated a fact or studied by science. Albert Einstein, who is considered one of the greatest minds ever, is attributed with the saying, "Imagination is more important than knowledge."

We often use the word *figment* alongside the word *imagination*. A figment is a fiction, fantasy, invention, or fable. My question is: How do we know that a figment doesn't exist as a truth in a simultaneous reality? In this culture we have been trained to be literal and sensible, and to think our perception of reality is the only one happening. Well, it is not. If we can get away from putting ourselves in the driver's seat of the Universe, we will have moments of knowing that allow us a vision of how vast the imagination of God is. After a few of these moments, we will never discount something as a simple figment again.

. . . .

PRACTICE IDEA: *Imagination and Truth*

When we allow ourselves to be more imaginative, life becomes more enchanting and engaging. What is wrong with having a story or a myth about why the sun comes up in the sky, or why we have seasons? Is there harm in telling children that a stork delivered them? Will they think you were a liar when they grow up and discover that the truth is a bit different? Truth is a funny thing. People often have their own version of the truth, which they may be quite attached to. What makes us believe something; is it the seeing, the touching, the written words? Take some time to consider what strikes your own truth bell.

There is a misconception about the imagination: If something exists only in our imagination, then we believe it is not based in truth, and therefore it should not affect us. The only way anything *could* affect us is through our imagination. We must come up with a story or a reference point in order to be affected, and this comes from the realm of imagination. The imagination is more than the act of being clever with ideas. We use our imagination to picture ourselves in relationship to the world around us. Practice using your imagination to create a new story about your life and your daily activities. Open yourself up and let the angels play along with you.

REFLECTING

THE WORLD

How hungry the human heart is for an image of
a Divine Mother that would, like an umbilical cord,
reconnect it to the Womb of Being, restoring the
lost sense of trust and containment in a dimension
that may be beyond the reach of our intellect,
yet is accessible to us through our deepest instincts.

—ANDREW HARVEY AND ANNE BARING

O UR PSYCHES HAVE A reflective quality when it comes
to the "Big Picture." We reflect what is happening
globally in a personal way. Think about the planet, the
globe, as a central psyche to which we are all linked. When
new information is fed into this global psyche, we are
affected, whether in a minute way or in a profound way.

Whenever there is a leap in technology, this is
reflected in our psyche. When a war breaks out over
conflicting beliefs or land rights, this sparks the energy of
our psyche. We can bring the picture in a little closer
and find that we reflect what is going on in our city, our

neighborhood, our family, and our home. This reflection shows up in unique ways in each of our lives, through dreams, art, and even the way we carry ourselves. The images can get scary when we think of all the things going on in the world that can be reflected in the mirror of our own psyche.

What do we do with the negative images and the overwhelming situations happening all over the globe? We seek a sense of balance in our own psyche, so that the negativity does not gain control. We keep our energy as healthy as possible by looking to Divine Providence. In this way we will have a healing imprint on the *anima mundi* — the world's soul.

Author Joseph Campbell wrote, "The spirit is not blown into man from without, but comes forth from the living of a noble heart; it's a quality of man himself." Most things considered divine have been sent off of the Earth throughout the course of history. Mary, the Divine Mother, is now a resident of the sky; the angels live in the clouds with God and Jesus. This is symbolic, and symbols are powerful and beautiful, but these symbols also possess a dark side. By removing all of our sacred values off of the Earth, we have disregarded the Earth, and failed to treat it as sacred. Out of our belief that this is merely our temporary home, we have taken on attitudes of usury in regard to the Earth's resources.

In the United States, we say we are a nation *under* God, not necessarily lower in stature, but down here taming the Earth for God so we can eventually join God up there, and share our penchant for killing off all the unholy things of the Earth. One part of the planetary mind seems to be at war with the Earth; the Earth seems to be viewed as an enemy we must tame and control, and we know it is not an easy kill. This is big trouble for those of us who want to integrate the sacred into our lives, because for a human the sacred is to be found and experienced here on Earth.

Why integrate the sacred into our lives and follow a spiritual path? Our soul might want us to live a spiritual life because it yearns for true communion with God and the angels. Our spirit may seek the means to soar toward the heavens. Our logical mind may tell us a spiritual path is good because good things come to us by good living. Our body may send us messages concerning what it needs by means of aches, pains, illnesses, and so on as a way of saying, "Be more conscious of the way you treat your temple."

Our heart and our etheric body are already connected to the Divine, but we can develop certain qualities that accelerate our spiritual growth and understanding of the divine. We may find that we sometimes get frustrated and wonder why anyone should bother with any of this. At times we may just want to run away to a mountaintop, sprout some wings, and take off. Just when we think that the absurdity has gone too far, we will meet an angel and realize Heaven is a place in our heart, and as a human we can create Heaven right here and now.

. . . .

PRACTICE IDEA: *Going Within*

We know things based on more than just a waking mind-set. We have a private world within us. Like miniature communication satellites, we constantly receive *and* give out information on both a conscious and unconscious level. The idea that the Kingdom of God is within means that the Divine lives within us in a distinctive and original way. The inner world is where our sacred space is discovered; it is where we till the soil and cultivate divine qualities.

Going within is a key to feeling whole and centered. Meditation, prayer, dream work, art, dancing, singing, chanting, daydreaming, and gardening are ways to the interior realms, where we can find rich treasures that strike awe in us at times. Choose one or more of these activities to practice going within. Don't cheat yourself;

what works for your inner journey may not be right for others. Spend some quality time within yourself. Of course, don't spend all your time within; the rest of us would like to see you once in a while! We must come out and share our gifts with the world once we discover them.

· 10 ·

FOR THE
LOVE OF GOD

Beloved, let us love one another, for love is
from God; and everyone who loves is born
of God and knows God. The one who does not love
does not know God, for God is love.

—1 JOHN 4:7–8

HAVE YOU EVER EXPERIENCED the powerful reactions that just the word *God* can bring about? I have seen hate wash over a person's face at just the mention of the word *God*. People who live in accordance with God, meaning they have had an experience of divine love and know how to share this love, hear the word *God* and a sense of peaceful understanding prevails. Other people may think that God gets in their way of truly having fun, or that they were forced into hearing about God, and as we know forcing is never good.

I challenge anyone who has ever been seized by the spirit of God and love to tell me they know of any better high attainable, or any better quality of fun. No drug you can take can ever compare with the amazing high achieved in the presence of the Lord's divine love. There is no level of sophistication worth attaining if it means giving up the down-home high of God. No matter how much esoteric knowledge I diligently seek to attain, I would throw it all out the window in one second if it got in the way of the pure, uncomplicated message of God I feel in my heart.

The energy of divine love is what will keep us on line with Heaven. Divine love lies behind all divinely charged qualities because love is God. Many people are asking themselves what on Earth this human experience is really all about. I often stop and wonder what I got myself into with this human birth. As one of my little research projects, I ask people what they think the human experience is really about. I ask all kinds of people, ranging in age, nationality, and gender, and the main answer I get is: "I may not be exactly sure what this is all about, yet I *know* our being here has something to do with love." I agree that our being here has everything to do with love. Love flows freely into our lives in the ways we allow it to. It knocks relentlessly on the doors we have closed off to it. Love, the ultimate divine quality, won't leave us alone.

The most powerful thing about love is that it is a flood of emotions, not just one tiny wave at a time. In other words, when your heart is opened wide by love, you may laugh and cry at the same time. We sometimes make a mistake and think that emotions are compartmentalized and that crying is too messy. I don't know about you, but I find about ten things to cry about each day. The greatest thing is that immediately following these ten impulses to cry is an impulse to laugh, hug someone, revel in joy, and so much more.

Another important thing to remember is that we do not need a perfectly healthy body in order to have deep experiences of love. Sometimes our most profound experiences of love may come when we are very sick. Granted, physical pain is no field day of fun, but it never means love is unavailable. The point is, there is no way to get ready for love, dress for love, or force love; you just need to be present, awake, and willing to let it go into action.

<hr />

God serves as an important healing force in the psyche when we come back to ourselves to figure things out. God has all the answers, and we have all the questions. God speaks to us by way of our heart (1 Samuel 16:7 "... for God sees not as man sees, for man looks at the outward appearance, but the Lord looks at the heart"), and that is where the struggle comes in. We want answers given to our intellect; we want them to be logical and absolute. Sometimes we happen upon an answer in a book, or we hear someone talk of answers to the great mysteries in life. But these answers don't always coincide with our actual experience of life; they are often in conflict with our passions and instincts. The answers look good on paper, and sound good to the intellect, but the mind only comes up with more questions. Only through the heart, through images and feelings evoked by symbols can we begin to understand life's mysteries.

Literal information about God, or literal information about anything for that matter, reaches the psyche and then must be "deliteralized," or stored in images and feelings. Images and feelings may eventually find a symbol to represent the information, but the symbol is not literal. The symbol is imaginal, which means it speaks to the imagination, which has a different set of values. No matter how hard we try to fit a spiritual concept into absolutes, we will always fail.

I believe we are at a very amazing point in the history of human consciousness. Ten years ago, when I wrote my first book, I had to argue with the publisher about referring to God as God, and not as the Great Spirit, or Mother Nature, or whatever was currently comfortable. Not long ago *God* was a taboo term outside of scripture-based Christianity. Now, our nonecumenical best-seller lists have titles with God in them regularly. A new reverence for the divine feminine encourages people to use "Mother/Father God" when addressing God in prayer. That just seems to feel right for our time.

I would like us to get past any leftover residue from the notion that God is dead, and accept the idea that we have an amazing gift we have been given called *life,* and we have it because God is not dead, and neither are we. We need to wake up from our sleepwalking. We have been hypnotized by too many things that tell us life is not wonderful just as it is. Our awareness comes from the light within us; to shine this light, to be awake, we cannot be dull and disconnected. If we dim out and sleepwalk because our beliefs tell us that life is too much about pain, then we will miss the experience of joy.

Truly awake people realize that there is a constantly changing continuum to life. If we step off the continuum, thinking that life is a disappointment, we miss the next moment when a small miracle can open our heart and take us far and beyond our personal pain. Let's snap out of the hypnotic gray area and follow the rainbow of light all around us.

God is alive — in our books, television shows, movies, and psyches. This does not mean everyone is interested in God, but you can't really miss God if you are a current reader or media watcher. If we took much of what we are fed about God *literally,* we would come to the conclusion that God is our best friend, a being to converse with; that God is not playing a big dice game in which humans are the aftermath; that God is not a "god" who manipulates us and plays tricks on us; and that God cares about us a lot — God is not careless. "God loves you; get over it," says Martha Williamson, producer of the television show *Touched by an Angel.*

Some people may think my feelings about God are puerile and politically incorrect, but this is not a concern for me at all. I think it is time for us to get past small problems like this. I am very willing to listen to others discussing their views and beliefs concerning God. I do not want to alter anyone's thinking about God; I only want to share inspiration that originates from my love of God.

We all have a private room in our psyches for God. Even when we don't believe in God, we have reasons tucked away in our psyche taking up energy and space to convince us that God doesn't exist. This can mean that a nonbeliever spends more time actually thinking about God than the average believer. When we are at a crossroads in life and don't know what to do, we can ask God for help. If we then listen to our heart, we will know what to do. Never think you are too sophisticated for God, because on some dark night you may really need God and then you will have to struggle with your sophisticated image and it will be harder to reach a breakthrough. However, when you do break through into the light of God's love, the struggle will be worth every second.

. . . .

PRACTICE IDEA: *Conveying Your Love of God*

There is, and always will be, a built-in problem with words and their limitations in conveying a concept, especially the concept of God. God and the angels, and indeed our very spiritual growth, are based on direct experience that goes beyond the mind, beyond words. When it is time to put our experience into words, we may feel stifled or frustrated that we cannot seem to recount the depth of our experience. That is why such beautiful art and music has been created throughout time to convey the experience of the Divine. Think of new ways you can convey your love for the Divine. You might want to write a poem, paint a picture, or simply visualize some artistic way of expressing your deepest love of God.

11

THE ETERNAL DELIGHT
OF GOD

Thou shalt not bore God.

—JOHN C. LILLY

"FOR WITH GOD NOTHING is ever impossible, and no word from God shall be without power or impossible of fulfillment," reads Luke 1:37 in the *Amplified Bible*. Reading something like this can touch us deeply, yet we humans continue to think along the same old lines, follow well-trodden paths, forget to have a sense of humor, and do untold other uninteresting things that have already been done. We are unique possibilities of God. When we heed the call to go on our spiritual path, we must remember to entertain God by entertaining new possibilities of love in our lives.

I have sometimes thought that another line should be added to the Beatitudes: Blessed are the entertaining, for they shall enjoy life. I doubt that God is delighted or entertained by humans who display brilliant minds and incredible creative talent, yet spend most of their time complaining about what they are not *getting* out of life, instead of finding new ways to manifest love. I'm sure the angels would rather look upon the Earth and see the glittering gold of spiritually awake people who are willing to love.

Have you ever noticed how delighted and entertained we are by movies that open our hearts, and give us a glimpse of how wonderful life can be when we grab that chance for happiness and love? If watching humans is like watching movies, then I think God and the angels are truly delighted and entertained each time we take a risk to love deeply and express our love creatively. Love is an energy of exchange; if we say that we love God yet do nothing about it, then we are expecting to receive love without giving it.

Let's look at the obvious: God and the angels are all about love, so if we want to attract divine energy into our lives, we need to *be* that love. The beautiful thing about *being love* is that it offers an original and divinely unique experience for each of us. No one else can tell us how to do it; the directions live in our heart. Just making one small move toward thinking of ourselves as entertaining to God can change our lives.

The best way to entertain the Great Creator and the angels is by using our ability to manifest an expression of love and open the door to a new possibility for others to do the same. At the end of our lives, we will be asked, "How well did you love?" What would your answer be today?

Being here on Earth is a great privilege, and our agreement in being here means that we are to be as interesting as possible to God. This doesn't mean we are to knock ourselves out trying to be successful on a grand level, and we don't need to become a superhero to be interesting. The most interesting thing we humans can do is discover who we are. Then we will realize that a divine force field of love is around us at all times. When we choose to let this field of love interact with our cells, we will be able to create unimaginable moments of beauty that will help heal the world's soul.

Gratitude is entertaining and always interesting to God. People with no gratitude or reverence for life often end up boring others with their complaints. Out of its intrinsic nature, gratitude is a truly unique way that we can express ourselves. When we choose to use our free will and our God-given right to think freely and to honor God, we have reverence for life. The key point here is that we choose to do this freely, on our own accord and in our own way.

The most sacred thing a human has is free will. This means that no matter what happens to us — short of losing the normal functions of our brain — we are able to choose how to behave, how to love, and how to use our free will. People often get mad at God because they were told to believe in God in an absolute way that just doesn't correspond with their experience of life. Using our free will to love God means that we don't have to swallow everything whole and choke on it.

Our job is to entertain God with our originality and deep understanding. God is entertained when we express who we truly are, because we are showing appreciation by using our gifts. Jesus spent time with sinners and tax collectors. He appreciated humor and beauty, and he lived in the moment. Saint Francis frolicked with the homeless and outcast. If the ship is sinking, let's get one last song in and sing along with God. It's time to dance on the tables and swing from the lights, and show Mother/Father God that no matter how doomed we feel, there is time to celebrate and express our appreciation of life.

· · · · · · · · · · · · · ·

PRACTICE IDEA: *Live in the Moment*

One basic spiritual truth that reemerges whenever we have exhausted all other efforts is to live in the moment. We have heard the sayings "Be here now," "Live as if this were your last day or hour," and "The only thing any of us have is right now." There are many other versions of this basic spiritual principle. Living in the present often brings up our issues about security, which we are very clever in trying to preserve. By "trying" to preserve something, however, we don't enjoy it. Let the angels be in charge of preserving life, joy, love, and beauty, and you can be in charge of showing up and enjoying it all. This way God will be entertained by your originality and innocence in meeting the moment as it is. Practice living in the moment.

12

Does God
"Hold Out"?

God is nearer to me than I am to my own self; my life
depends on God's being near to me, present in me.
So He is also in a stone, a log of wood, only they
do not know it. If the wood knew of God and realized
His nearness like the highest angel does, then the
log would be blessed as the chief of all the angels.
Man is more happy than a log of wood in that he
knows and is aware of God, how near at hand God is.
—MEISTER ECKHART

I F WE TREAT GOD like a cosmic parent who had better give us what we want or we will cause a tantrum, then we will be like children who don't know any better. If you had children who you kept giving beautiful jewels to, and they wanted friends and power so much that they would turn around and give the jewels to people who would go off and leave your children with nothing, would you continue to give your children jewels? Probably not. How would you feel if you were a parent who put beautiful food on the table every night, but your children kept going to the neighbor's for crumbs because they had an extreme fascination with the neighbor and so they settled for crumbs? Then, to add extra insult, the children blamed the parent for their starvation.

Sometimes we blame God for our unhappiness, such as when we convince ourselves that another human we have *"fallen* in love" with is our savior, or we are his or hers. There is certainly a fine line here, and you need God every step of the way if you think you are here to save another person's soul. Each human relationship is unique, and I am not so bold as to speak for God in these matters, but I have never seen anyone prove successful in taking responsibility for another person's salvation or happiness. I have seen people be present in love for another, with the true consciousness of God and love and compassion, and the relationship has become a healing one. A healing relationship is not based on power or control; it is based on love and mutual respect. What good does it do anyone if you give love, lavish gifts, and spend all your daydreaming and prayer time on a person who simply does not have love for you? There are plenty of takers of this one-way love, so please be careful if you truly want to be happy.

When you find happiness in your own backyard, in what you have, and in the inner gifts you are given, then you truly "have it all." If you find someone who also has that same kind of happiness, and together you choose to share it, then you possess one of God's greatest, most magnificent gifts. But God can only give if we are able to receive and be *entrusted* with God's gifts. If we keep using the gifts to control and demand, they will no longer be gifts.

God has all the love in the world for us. We need to trust God and let go of any need for power and control over others, or for another human to worship us. God doesn't love us through another human. God loves us directly. When we have a heart full of love, we can share this with another human whose heart is also full of love, knowing and honoring where original love comes from.

I had a friend who in the pain and frustration of not getting what he wanted — a relationship with someone who was not available — claimed that "God is weak and cannot overcome the opposing forces." In all my life I had never heard anyone say something like that before, and I must say I was stunned. First, of course, this is a grand projection, because he was weak in the moment. Second, how does God get strength? We can help, when we stop creating hell on Earth by trying to be God, or trying to be in competition with God by controlling every situation.

Have you ever thought about what happens when you *get what you want*? Usually, you don't realize the exact moment it has happened, and getting what you want often comes when you have been focusing on something else, so it doesn't hold the great importance you once gave it. If the object of what you want is another person, that person usually "gives in" just when you see that who you have been projecting all of these grand illusions on is simply another human with many faults just like you, someone who couldn't save you any more than the next person.

God is love. Love is a behavior and an energy that needs to move. Love is at its highest form when we are giving it and feel blessed for the chance to give. Where there is a power struggle, love is not the fuel. If love is given only under strict conditions, beware of what is going on. If you think you can only love a certain person in a certain situation, or someone who looks a certain way, then you may attract someone who can meet your standards and conditions. That person may get your love because they are worthy of it and can play the game, but what will you get?

When we play in the eternal fields of consciousness and acknowledge that we are much more than the small point of awareness we refer to as our waking mind, then we will want to think beyond our limited beliefs and dogma. I don't mean that we are called to ridicule anything that comes to us by way of belief, but we are wise to look at it more deeply, feel it, be open to expansion, and ask the angels for a transcended view.

One of my all-time favorite movie scenes is when the Wizard of Oz is fumbling around with his projection screen equipment and is caught, then says, "Pay no attention to the man behind the curtain." If you are seeking a human wizard for information, remember that he or she is only human. If you happen to see the person behind the image, be forgiving and enjoy the humor. God works in mysterious ways and may choose to bring a trickster into our lives to create a transformation within us.

. . . .

PRACTICE IDEA: *Laughter*

The word *illusion* comes from the Latin word *illudere,* meaning to mock and make fun of. Sometimes there seems to be an unkind force in the Universe that is out to mock us. The more upset we become, the more it gains power over us. But if we find humor in our situation and have the first laugh, this force is rendered powerless. Practice having the first laugh *and* the last laugh too. The angels will join you and the light of truth will dispel the illusions. Seeing life through the eyes of humility will give you a new sense of meaning that is based more on truth and less on illusory images. Above all, just live with the intention of having laughter in your life.

13

RADICAL FREEDOM

Freedom here does not mean being wild or sloppy;
rather it is letting yourself go so that you
fully experience your existence as a human being.

—CHÖGYAM TRUNGPA

How do we know when we are free? Is freedom a feeling, an image, or mostly a state of mind, which doesn't necessarily depend on the physicality of our situation? What is a free spirit? Can you be free in prison? Is freedom an illusion? Does it always have a price? Is discipline the opposite of freedom or its necessary companion?

Some people run around cutting ties, making sure they have no responsibilities, and then proclaim they are free. Some of us think that having a lot of money will lead us to freedom. Others base their freedom on acquiring knowledge and understanding. There are people who think that the right to keep guns is the ultimate expression of freedom. Some people allow themselves to be extremely self-indulgent as an act of freedom. The perception of freedom is quite individualized.

The bottom line is that many people have not incorporated a true sense of freedom in their consciousness and become free spirits, happy to present themselves to the world just the way they are. Instead, people today seem almost paralyzed with fear concerning who they are, what they look like, and whether they are doing the right thing. Where are all the eccentrics and other people who are willing to just have fun and include everyone in it? The angels have trouble getting noticed when people are excessively self-conscious and worried more about controlling their lives than letting go and having fun.

When considering the current group consciousness, I think we need to collectively lighten up and be more creative. There are too many critics in the kitchen. Instead of finding ways to lighten up and heal society, we seem to be searching for more conspiracy theories, more people to punish, and more fear-born causes to pull us down. Too many people are ready to draw their spiritual guns at the slightest provocation. Collectively we encourage intense emotional dramas, instead of natural ways to ease the stress and fear of life.

We are a part of what goes on in the collective psyche, whether or not we are consciously contributing to it. So we need the angels to help us find our own way to radical freedom. *Radical* means fundamental, basic, and carried to the farthest extreme or limit. Etymologically, *radical* means "of roots," coming from the Latin *radicalis,* which means having roots. We have used the word *radical* to describe those who support revolutionary changes in politics or government, stemming from the idea of "fundamental" change — going to the roots of things. What does freedom have to do with roots? Roots are alive; they bring us good things from down under. When we have our own roots, based on our own truths and heart, then we have freedom.

Part of the bargain in having this sacred chance to be alive is that the life of our body will end at some point. This point of departure is a mystery; it is God's domain, and no matter how much we may try to control life, humans simply cannot explain death. Death is so mysterious and it can seem so painful that people feel the need to explain it, to say why someone may have died young, or why someone got cancer, or had a heart attack. By explaining what happened to others, we can say in our minds, "That won't get me!" And how do we explain people who keep living and rendering these explanations moot by smoking, drinking, and eating a lot of high-fat food? How do we explain someone who has made a serious effort to live healthy in body and mind, yet still gets cancer?

When we humans face death during an extended illness or other serious circumstance, my guess is that we don't look back on our lives and say, "Oh darn, I wish I had worked longer hours and acquired more things," or "If only that money-making scam had worked." The truth is that we may wish we had watched more sunsets with our loved ones, played a little longer with our children or pets, danced more, sang more, and listened more closely to the angels. The gift is that death is always present, and reminds us that the message of radical freedom is speaking to us now.

The angels want us to stop trying to cheat death with illusions of security. Radical freedom means moving away from the impulse to seek security at any price. Radical freedom directs us to go back to the root causes of our self-imprisonment and look for the wisdom of the reality of death, not the security blanket of denial.

When we find ourselves in a "dark night of the soul" brought on by loss and we choose to stay awake in the dark, the issue of our mortality will find its way into our pain, and we will meet death face-to-face. At first the reality of death may cause us to tremble with fear, and then our focus may shift and we will come to accept loss. We will let all of it go; everything comfortable we have been hanging onto is being taken away from us, and we are letting it happen.

A dark night of the soul is a mystical experience. In the course of our pain, we may happen upon the idea that perhaps death can save us from all of this pain and overwhelming loss, but then a voice from the depths of our soul says, "No, death will not save us; it is time to get up and fight for life." Time to get up and stand in the fire and let your life force lead the way. The angels will be there as midwives, not to remove you from the pain of new birth, but to assist in the birth, allowing you to go through the labor until you awaken in the morning in the new light of sacred consciousness that will infuse your soul with strength and radical freedom.

A "dark night" may take only one moment of this type of connection with your soul, or it may take weeks and then repeat itself. The dark night of the soul is not out to *get* you; it is out to *give* you real life and radical freedom. There are no rules or steps for facing the pain in your life. There are no New Age formulas for cheating the pain or taking a shortcut. The angels want you to have the gift of real life, and that takes real courage. The illusions fade when you ask for truth. This is the way of radical freedom: Let the illusions fade so you can clearly see what gifts of life are really yours.

. . . .

PRACTICE IDEA: *Radical Freedom*

Have a conversation with God and ask all the questions you may have about the mystery of death and loss. Write down what God would tell you in a moment of pain and loss. Write until you feel the truth dancing its way out of you; write until you sense your part in the angelic harmony of the Universe and can feel your fire joining in with the cosmic fire. Write until the sacred sound from your beating heart is in tune with the highest choir of singing angels. Be with yourself and your pain until your soul is floating in the water of life, held safe and sound in the womb of love. God bless your failures and your losses; look what they have brought you.

· 14 ·

OPENING
OUR MINDS

Maat, Goddess of Justice, weighs human hearts
at the end of life. If they are lighter than
a feather, they can move on to the afterlife.
If they are too heavy, they return to Earth.
—EGYPTIAN MYTH

WE CAN TALK ABOUT FREEDOM as if it's something we have an advanced degree in, but I think most people have a fear of true freedom. Some of us are desperately afraid of alternative lifestyles, "different" people, and new experiences. I once knew a white man who owned a shop in a racially mixed neighborhood in the South. More than once I observed him when business was slow, sitting on the porch with a black man laughing and talking up a storm. In fact, I rarely saw the two of them quite so animated in other situations. They brought the best out in each other. Then at the end of the day, they went home and returned to their racist talk and behavior. I would hear the white man saying incredibly racist things, and I would think of the way he spent many of his days. Our life experiences are what really count, and if we could go out into the world free from archaic, discriminatory, or judgmental beliefs, we would be better able to experience life in a more honest and beautiful way. We would learn how to treat situations as unique instead of lumping them into big categories based too often on hate, ignorance, fear, and media hype.

If you have no trust in humanity and you think everyone is out to get you, for whatever reason, you will fit situations into this belief. Humans are very clever at attracting ways to manifest their fears. When we are willing to listen to the impulses and warning bells the angels ring in our hearts, we will attract fewer of life's bad experiences. We have all the talent we need to manifest a sense of peace and freedom deep within us and to share this with others. Eventually if we let go of the black-and-white, either/or way of thinking, we will come to see the "bad" experiences in a completely new light and we may find enough spiritual strength to transmute it to good. This way we will be on track for wonderful blessings, and a collection of great stories to share.

Letting ourselves ask questions instead of insisting on having all the answers is one way to begin to open our minds.

Question Break

If you have an opinion, does this mean it has to be the right opinion?

If someone has a different opinion, is it wrong?

How do you know if you are open-minded? Have you tested yourself on this?

What happens when you meet someone you really like, but that person's opinions clash with yours?

Are your opinions sanctioned by the angels and God?

What if one of your opinions was to change dramatically within minutes of hearing something new?

Have you ever really thought about what an opinion is?

. . . .

PRACTICE IDEA: *Freedom from Stifling Beliefs*

Consider the following ideas about overcoming spells, superstitions, and stifling beliefs and reclaiming your true freedom:

Free Yourself from Superstition

Because life is such a risky business, we come up with many little games to play in order to fool ourselves into thinking we have a semblance of control over things. Superstition is one game we play, and we are all very creative with it. From chain letters to lucky numbers, from depending on a lucky charm or fortunate aspect in our horoscope to the psychic hotline, it is time for us to begin to let go of our superstitions. The trouble with superstitions is that they can get in the way of our angel consciousness and impede our quest for radical freedom.

Break the Spell

The word *spell* originates from the Old English word for story. A story is very powerful, but don't forget it is flexible; it can be rearranged and told differently. Traditionally a spell is an incantation, a formula, or a bewitched state. Think about the idea of a human under the spell of something. What comes to mind? When we think of people being under a spell, we mean that something other than their own free will is influencing their path in life. So right here we realize the angels are not being heard. Spells play havoc in our psyche, and they come from beliefs that we rarely stop and analyze, since we are unaware of them.

Don't Retire

Free yourself from the idea that certain things must happen to us as we get older. If we go along with the usual story of aging in our society, we will believe — and it will come to pass — that our sexuality will end, our mind will become dull, our body will totally give out on us, we will not be beautiful anymore, and we may end up in a nursing home. This is a very sad story, and it does not have to come true. Of course we change as we age, and that is beautiful if we accept the changes and do our best. I met a woman a few years ago, when she was 104 years old. She is not only very attractive, but extremely creative and alive. Her sensuality is still very much a part of her, and the light in her eyes is as bright as a child's. Now why wouldn't we opt for that story instead of the fear story?

Don't ever get old and retire! *Retirement* is one of the worst words ever invented. It means to withdraw, depart, resign, and remove from a career. The word *tire* originally meant fail, cease, come to an end; "become weary" is a secondary meaning. "Re" means back again. Re-tire? Back again to fail, cease, resign, withdraw, and depart from life. Only God knows when we depart from "life." If we are going to invent an age marker for such a negative idea like retirement, we are cheating ourselves out of the best part of our life.

Leap Off the Wheel

A belief that we are working off past-life karma can choke us when we start experiencing the rewards and punishment we believe are connected to it. I don't want to get into a debate about whether reincarnation and karma are true. That is up to each of us personally. The concept of reincarnation is interesting and can lend itself to some deep self-exploration, *but* when the past-life stories start to overshadow present life, I have found this to be incompatible with angel consciousness. All the angels ask is that you find your own divinity. This takes you out of the wheel of karma, because when you change your character, you change your destiny; so don't short-change yourself!

Don't Let Astrology Get You Down

Another area that we can get caught up in is astrological spells, limitations, and predictions. I happen to think astrology is interesting from a mythic aspect, and can help us keep in mind how absurd the gods can be. However, I am very disappointed that it seems to be so masculine oriented. When you look at the names of the planets used to chart a human course, you find only one planet, Venus, named after a goddess. What if Saturn had been named Athena; Mars named Hera? The male orientation may be one reason why so many astrological predictions and transiting explanations can seem so harsh and unforgiving. The divine masculine commands, "Thou shalt," while the divine feminine reminds us, "Thou mayest," meaning we are allowed to change, we are permitted to be happy, and we are sanctioned to be loved. Thou mayest be yourself.

· 15 ·

LIVE AND
LET LIVE

Our responsibility — our capacity to respond to
the challenges that face us, our response ability —
is to reconnect with the larger Source that we
sometimes call divine. When we do so, we reconnect
with the energy and the plan for our larger life and
all that it entails. . . . We are as different as snowflakes,
and our ways to the Source reflect this.

—JEAN HOUSTON, *A Passion for the Possible*

I THINK JUNGIAN ANALYST Marion Woodman is one of the most inspiring people around. She once told a story of when she had just come through a treacherous encounter of "battling" cancer and she was at a party with great music. She has always loved to dance, and the music was calling to her. She was obviously in a weakened state, but she got herself up and started to move. Her husband was a little worried and didn't want her to dance, but she knew she had to do it for life.

What is our first impulse when those close to us need to move, break free from convention, or express themselves?

Is the first instinct to stop them, in case they say something weird or make a fool out of themselves? Why do we seem to have this compulsive need to keep others from "hurting themselves," when it may be the very thing that could heal them?

Why do we sometimes resent people who are being themselves and are proud of it? What makes people so uncomfortable around free spirits? We send many mixed messages out into the world, especially to children. We tell them to feel good about themselves, and then when they express themselves from the core of their being, we try to control it. Maybe this leads to neurosis, where instead of people sharing their heart's inspiration, they suppress their creativity and express the neurotic behavior instead.

In *The Alchemy of Prayer,* I wrote about the aboriginal approach to "dreamstealing." Dreamstealing is when others tells us of their dreams, goals, or desires to do something, and we answer back with hits to the psyche, such as, "Oh, that is impossible," or "Who do you think you are?" or "You have no talent for that." I have heard that in certain tribes if people are caught in the act of dreamstealing, they get the bone pointed at them, which means they are banished from existence, the worst punishment possible in that society. Dreamstealing is so prevalent in our own society that it happens almost unconsciously. It can even be conveyed with a quick look or gesture.

Another area in which we steal the chance for other people's greatness is when we steal their pain. What if we keep others from experiencing what we have decided is a painful situation, but it turns out to be the one time they might have reached a moment of truth in their soul, hear the angels, and discover their true path after the dark night of pain? We also project a great deal of pain on the experience of failure. The funny thing is that if we label something or someone a failure, we are the ones experiencing the pain. The people we have deemed to have failed may be having rich experiences of truth and beauty, which will lead to a success far greater than the world knows. They may be discovering new heights of creativity with the angels. To quote the truly independent and brilliant filmmaker John Sayles, "I run into people all the time who are paralyzed by the fact that they might fail. To me, there's no failure. This is all an exploration."

. . . .

PRACTICE IDEA: *Live and Let Live*

Living is something we do, not something we talk about. When the music starts, join in and don't worry what people think, or whether someone is going to get hurt. Be a "permissionary." Imagine how sad the angels would be if we stopped others from being their true selves .in the moment, and kept them from an experience which would help us all find our way. Take a day and consciously give others permission to be themselves, to go as far as they need to go. During this day review your ideas about success. How do you know when people are "successful" in life? How do you know when you have attained "success?" What criteria are you using in your judgments? Let go of them, and live and let live.

16

ACCEPTING
VARIED REALITIES

The deeper the Self-realization of a man,
the more he influences the whole universe by
his subtle spiritual vibrations and the less
he himself is affected by the phenomenal flux.

—PARAMAHANSA YOGANANDA'S MASTER

B EING HUMAN IS AN amazing and challenging experience, to say the least. When I contemplate the myriad possibilities of human realities on God's green Earth, I find myself facing a great challenge. For example, one Sunday I found the following in the newspaper: First I noticed a picture of a woman bent over a couple of large duffel bags with a look of despair on her face. She had missed boarding the only train of the day leaving her war-torn city. The next thing that caught my eye was the picture of an elder college professor in front of his beautiful home, on what he described as "the worst day of his life" — the day a ninety-year-old oak tree had to be removed from his front yard. Then in another section of the paper was the account of a camp that meets once a year for children with cancer. They discuss losing their hair and the cruel names they have been called, such as "baldy" or "leukemia master." They talk about the phone call that made their parents break down and cry.

After scanning the newspaper, I was overcome by the challenge of accepting all these varied realities. At any moment in time, babies are being born, and people are dying. Happy moments are transpiring, and tragedies are developing. One man pushes the remains of his expensive dinner away as he waits for his dessert, while another starves in poverty searching the city dumpsters for an evening meal. This world is full of so many amazing scenarios happening simultaneously. How do we choose the reality we want to live in, make it okay to be in it, and then do our best to help others who are less fortunate? It takes awareness, awakeness, hope, and acceptance of a higher purpose in life.

When I ask the angels for answers to the human mystery, I find that they guide me to a sense of peace and comfort in my soul. The angels do this not by bringing me answers and intricate theories, but by bringing me creative ways of responding to life with light in my heart. The angels help me to keep hope alive when nothing makes sense. Making sense and solving the mystery becomes less important when the angels are present in our lives. Life doesn't have to make sense according to a human viewpoint of right and wrong, good and bad.

If we are to understand even one moment of life, we need to constantly position ourselves for a new view. We need to look at, look around, look under, look through, look in, and look sideways at things. The angels help me do this. When I begin to take something too seriously, I stop and imagine what it would look like from the angels' perspective. I don't know God's ultimate plan, but I do know that having reverence for life is wise. I also know that if I stop focusing so much energy on the futility of explaining things and taking everything apart with my limited analytic mind, then I have more time to spend on the bigger picture. When I get to this level, thanks to the angels, I truly feel like a free spirit able to navigate wisely in the world.

The end of this millennium, as I mentioned earlier, is making some people very fearful. Many people think that the reason the angels are making themselves more visibly present is that the world is nearing an end. Part of this fear may be based on the atrocities that are happening in the world. Even if we haven't been directly responsible for some atrocity, we know it's wrong to allow them to continue. The atrocities are splitting our psyche. We may have recently found real ways to be happy and peaceful within ourselves, but we listen to a discussion on the radio and find out that the shoes we are wearing are assembled by workers in Indonesia who are treated like slaves. They are only earning one dollar a day in abusive conditions, yet the shoe company is able to pay a sports celebrity $20 million to represent them in a few commercials. I don't know about you, but this kind of thing saddens my heart.

I could rant on about widespread corporate disregard of human rights, but that is not my goal in this book. My goal is that we wake up and understand ourselves more, and to do this we have to see the whole picture, and realize that there are a myriad of realities going on. It is not fun to live with a split psyche. You may feel the need to stop wearing shoes made by companies who mistreat their workers, you may decide to boycott certain products, or you may feel called upon to speak out against the craziness you see. The Dalai Lama has said, "The primary aim of all religions is to help people become better human beings. Therefore, whatever our personal beliefs, it is more important to try to create a safer, kinder world than to attempt to recruit more people to the religion that happens to satisfy us. From my own experience I have found the greatest degree of inner tranquillity comes from the development of love and compassion."

. . . .

PRACTICE IDEA: *Kindness and Compassion*

If each of us took care of the deficit of kindness and compassion in a small way, we would make a big change. If we took the time to think about how our actions, thoughts, and intentions really look to the angels, and then changed our behavior to be in alignment with Spiritual Law, we would be helping the angels more than we could ever imagine. I don't think we are asked to be saints in the old-fashioned way. We are asked to do something even more difficult: to enjoy life and continue loving in the face of turmoil and confusion, while watching old structures we depended on fall to the ground.

We know instinctively that the world has a very dark side, and the darker it gets, the brighter the light becomes in contrast. Both dark and light are available to humans. If we choose to evolve into the light, it will be done, and we will be available for the special grace given to beings brave enough to *be here now*. This grace means we can enjoy life, laugh often, and make our life a dance, instead of a difficult climb to something forever out of our reach. It means we will, in the face of all adversity, finish a creative project even though it makes no sense because we see it as an important expression of life. Wherever life is being expressed in loving creative ways, the angels are there in flocks. Wherever humans are, there are angels.

17

THE SPIRIT
OF HUMOR

The devil may act like a trickster,
show wit, play the clown, dance a jig, and
be a jokester, but the humus and humility of
humor — never! . . . *The laughing recognition*
of one's own absurdity in the human comedy
bans the devil as effectively as garlic and the cross.

—JAMES HILLMAN

HAVE YOU EVER LAUGHED so hard you could hardly stop yourself? Think about the powerful feeling of joy and freedom that this brings. The real spirit of humor is a direct experience of divine bliss. Some of the best angel experiences I have had included humor so pure that those of us involved were laughing and crying from our souls. Instead of being quiet and fearful when something embarrassing happens, think of how much better it is when the spirit moves those involved to have a good laugh at human foibles. Researchers have found that many people whom we consider evil, such as the leaders of the

Nazi party during World War II, had no sense of humor. For them, no joy was found in laughter, and anything that ventured outside the lines of their structured evil minds was anything but funny.

One afternoon I was in a sushi bar with a friend, drinking hot sake and talking about life, philosophy, and intense emotions such as anger. As we talked I looked around at the numerous stunning masks decorating the walls, in a line encompassing the whole room. The masks were "demonic" looking, and most of them wore laughing or mocking expressions. The napkin had the restaurant logo on it, and I kept wondering what the name of this restaurant meant, since right next to the name was, of course, a demonic-looking mask. My friend and I got into a discussion about what happens when we are facing people full of anger, and they are letting it fly in our face. I said that at those times it was as if the demons are laughing at us, and if *we* laugh — if we refuse to take their spew personally, then we rise above the situation, and the whole alchemy changes. The lights come on, and the demons scatter. At that moment the waiter came to the table, and I asked him what the name of the restaurant meant and he answered, "The Demons Are Laughing."

The noted psychologist Carl Jung is often quoted as saying, "The only divine quality humans possess is humor."

If you regularly laugh and find humor, then you are well balanced in your attitude toward life. If you find that your sense of humor is a bit lacking and you are taking things too seriously, this is an important signal to make some changes in your life. Pay attention and laugh; this is paramount to your relationship with the angels, because they have a marvelous sense of humor and want to share it with you.

Let us keep sacred the fact that we have the choice to take life lightly. Most of the things we are so stressed out about just aren't serious in the big scheme of life as a vital part of the *anima mundi,* the soul of the world. There is no doubt that certain situations call for seriousness, but we don't have to be extra heavy about it and get stuck in a sinkhole of depression. We can change our seriousness into acute awareness, and give ourselves fully to the moment. This way humor will share the stage.

When we are authentic, there is no risk of humor trivializing a serious situation. I have encountered all kinds of situations that seemed to call for seriousness, yet each time humor came to pay its kindly visit. I have experienced major earthquakes, two firestorms that nearly reached my front door, a hurricane that required immediate evacuation, family accidents and tribulations. There is no doubt that these events are among the most serious, when energy is focused on survival. But some wonderful things started to dance around in my consciousness during the most crucial moments, such as a recognition of how precious life is, how immaterial most of our material things are, how short life is, how amazing love is, and how a prayerful moment of silence with God can center me more quickly than anything known to humankind.

. . . .

PRACTICE IDEA: *Good Humor*

Make an effort to ask the angels for a good laugh, and then be willing to really "go for it." The laughter may strike in a way you don't expect, which is often the best form of humor. Prepare yourself for a good laugh by learning how to relax and de-stress. The world is not out to get you. Think about ways to tune into the natural, simple ways of living, such as walking barefoot, talking to God, talking to plants, making believe, daydreaming, tai chi, yoga, and other forms of de-stressing. Practice living in a Zen-like manner, especially when you are driving. If you are living in God time, you always get to your destination right on time. Think about God having a sense of humor. And remember, "Angels can fly because they take themselves lightly."

· 18 ·

RESTORING BALANCE
THROUGH RITUAL

*All a ritual does is concentrate your mind on the
implications of what you are doing. For instance, the
marriage ritual is a meditation on the step you are taking
in learning to become a member of a dyad, instead of one
individual all alone. The ritual enables you to make the
transit. Ritual introduces you to the meaning of what's
going on. Saying grace before meals lets you know that
you're about to eat something that once was alive.*

—JOSEPH CAMPBELL

RITUAL IS ONE OF those words that some people react
to quite strongly. Some people may be afraid of performing rituals, thinking that only witches and ill-mean-
ing people use them. Others may feel that only a priest or
clergyperson can conduct a ritual. We do not honor rituals or rites as our ancestors did, although this is beginning
to change. People are looking for meaning in their lives
and a balance between the sacred and the profane. With
rituals we can acknowledge and honor an important
change we are about to make in our lives. Ritual is being
restored to its rightful place.

Most of us perform little rituals throughout our day. Remember, a ritual is something done to restore balance, and the changing nature of life itself demands that we seek balance. Balance may not be a completely realistic goal, since things change so quickly, but coming back to a sense of balance is very important for humans.

Think about your day. You wake up, and I bet you do pretty much the same thing each morning. And, when you are not able to do it, you may feel a bit off kilter. For example, brushing your teeth is a ritual action that helps to restore your balance as well as clean your teeth. Having a cup of coffee or a cigarette can also be a ritual. Children naturally perform little rituals when they are left to play freely. Years ago, I was the guardian of an afternoon day care center and loved to watch as the children played uninterrupted. Often they would reenact very mythic themes with little rituals, using berries, feathers, branches, and whatever else was on hand. Very likely you played this way as a child. We are naturally drawn toward mythic themes, and if we don't express them in play or art, we watch soap operas and talk shows in which people are living out archetypal themes of betrayal, competition, and unrequited love.

Consider how you personally restore balance or comfort in your life on a regular basis. I want you to get comfortable with the word *ritual*. We are getting too superstitious and fearful of things that can help us to live a more balanced and natural life; we are allowing opportunities for ritual to pass us by that may actually divert personal and societal problems. We need to get over some of the ridiculous limits we impose on ourselves.

Sometimes the angels call us to a situation where we may be the ones to initiate a balancing ritual. My friend Jai lives an inner-directed life, on call for the angels, so many great stories emanate around her. She is also not afraid to create a ritual to restore balance in a given situation. A good friend of Jai's, Sally, died a few years ago, and Sally's mother sent Jai a beautiful little silver jar with some of Sally's ashes. I was visiting Jai at the time, and she said she wanted to do something special to honor Sally and scatter her ashes in a place she loved, but didn't have any idea what to do. I suggested we go up to the top of a beautiful mountain that overlooks a valley and let our inner guidance lead us. So we gathered some necessary items: a candle, some incense, a bottle of red wine, and Jai's flute, and went off to our designated spot, gathering wildflowers on the way. We came to a little bench and set up our sacred space by lighting the candle, placing the flowers around, and then sitting in meditation while Jai played her flute.

When Jai was ready, she walked to the edge of the hill and began to free the ashes. A gentle but firm breeze was blowing, the sun was playing games with the clouds, and as the ashes scattered the lighter ones caught the breeze and made a beautiful exit upward, catching the sunlight, while the heavier ones landed quietly on the Earth. This experience was symbolic of our reality as humans, for we are both spirit moving upward and flesh made from the Earth. I started singing to God as the ashes went out to help the spirit find its way home. After this, we opened our wine and toasted Sally. We then toasted the Mother Earth who gave us the wine. We went to the mountain not knowing exactly what we would do, but by letting our intentions lead us, we spontaneously created a beautiful ritual that helped restore the balance of death and life.

Just last night Jai called and told me how she had been called up to the house of a well-known woman who was dying, to do hospice work. The night before receiving the call about the woman, Jai had had a vivid dream about this woman dying and had woken up with a deep, peaceful feeling. When she arrived a little early for a meeting of the hospice workers, she went in to visit her friend and within minutes she died. The people in the house went into a whirlwind of confusion; they didn't know what to do first. So Jai, with her gift of spontaneous ritual, started to direct everyone to restore the balance in the room by creating an altar with candles and flowers. She then suggested several other things that naturally restored the whirling energy into a sacred space where people could be present and able to respond with calm and peacefulness.

Don't take ritual too seriously, but remember that if you are helping the angels — and most likely you are or you wouldn't be reading this book — then be ready for the call to restore balance with a spontaneous ritual. All that's needed is to open your heart to the divine beat of the Universe, let go of any need to control, or any desire for personal gain, and you will know what to do.

Please note, "just for the record," that I am not promoting "ritual magic" or witchcraft, which is sometimes performed with the intent to create an *imbalance* by throwing the outcome in the doer's favor. As the writer Manly P. Hall notes, a "sorcerer is a person who attempts by some special art to divert the forces of nature to his own personal ends. The true purpose of metaphysics is to perfect the inner self in wisdom, virtue, and understanding. All forced growth is sorcery."

The darkest side of sorcery is that unfortunately some people think it's their duty to put a curse on other people, or punish them by putting them under a spell. This is an expression of hatred, which when sent out, acts like a boomerang that comes right back to the person who sent it. But it can do harm to someone, especially if that person is having a difficult and fearful time. Acting from a place of hatred is unwise, and among other things, reflects great ignorance. Even when people attempt to right the wrong of an injustice by punishing another, they don't know the many particulars of the injustice, including the possibility of actual innocence. This can only cause more harm, not justice. I say leave it up to God's divine will, and all things will come out in the big cosmic washing machine. If indeed a wrong has been perpetrated, the outcome will be much more satisfying, since God has a great imagination and sense of humor.

. . . .

PRACTICE IDEA: *Using Rituals*

One aspect of ritual entails *registering* something in our consciousness that will become an integral part of our evolving spiritual insight. Some meanings of the word *register* include record, enter, inscribe, list, archive, manifest. Be careful of the thoughts and beliefs you register and bring to life. Sometimes we may register the opposite of what we want, such as negative beliefs, without our full awareness. Are your thoughts and beliefs helping you, hindering you, or allowing a free flow of illumination? Perform a ritual today that says, "Yes, God, I will get out of the way, and let your will be done."

What to Register with a Ritual
>   Goals
>   Dreams and daydreams
>   Fantastic images
>   Powerful ideas
>   Noble thoughts
>   Rants and raves
>   Gratitude
>   Compassion

Natural Rituals
>   Praying
>   Singing (or listening to music)
>   Dancing (or drumming)
>   Painting
>   Walking
>   Writing (including nonsense poetry)
>   Meditating and contemplating
>   Shrine or altar building

19

PEACE AND
QUIET

Trust yourself in the deep, uncharted waters. When there
is a storm, it is safer in the open sea. If you stay
too near the dock, you will get beaten to death.
—HOWARD THURMAN

W HEN THE ANGELS CAME into my life, one of the first
things I set out to deal with was my tendency to
worry. I am still dealing with this tendency, and perhaps I
always will be, but I can say the angels have given me
insight into ways to get back to my center after too much
worrying. The above quote by Howard Thurman is a good
start. Don't stay too near the dock and batter yourself
with worry. Worrying is what keeps us attached to the
dock, causing us to get bruised and battered in the storm
of life. If something is keeping you up nights or haunting
your days with worry, the best thing to do is distance

yourself from the situation. This is not always easy to do; if we are worrying about something, then we think we can control it by keeping it close to us. Yet we know what happens when we get too close to something; we are not able to see the big picture. If we could see the big picture, the one the angels view, then our worries would look small.

The word *worry* originally meant strangle or choke; it emerged in the sixteenth century as a term for harassing physically, coming from the notion of "seizing by the throat." By the seventeenth century, it meant to vex and disturb, then eventually came to mean mental uneasiness and anxiety. When we are mentally uneasy and anxious, it can feel as if we are being choked.

It is important to make a distinction between thinking about something, such as pondering a decision, and worrying about the same thing. Worry brings with it the issue of control. If we are worrying, we may feel we lack control of a situation, and are engaged in an inner battle. Worry competes with our faith and hope. To have faith and hope in a natural way means we feel comfortable and at ease. Worry makes us uncomfortable; it creates physical *dis-* ease and makes us feel as if our whole body was being choked and cut off from the divine stream of energy.

Worrying often seems like an endless loop, with the worry playing its message over and over in our mind. Each time we hear the message, it may seem to be gaining power, like that proverbial snowball rolling down the hill, getting bigger and bigger. What starts as a simple thought, can inadvertently gain momentum by collecting more and more evidence in its favor. At some point we have to get out of the way of the snowball and learn to change the outcome of a situation by letting go of the worry. This is where the angels are important allies. They can see us as light and love, and when they look at us full of worry, they urge us to be aware of what the worry is doing and then offer us ways to change it.

Often worry has to do with excessive pride, or taking things too personally. When we have taken something personally and feel dishonored by another, we may worry about restoring our dignity or honor. Well, this is a trap, because no one should be allowed to have so much power over us that they can take away our dignity. Think about it. Why do the words *foolish* and *pride* go together so well? Worrying about what others think is so futile that it could be seen as foolish. You cannot control another person's perception of you *ever,* no matter how hard you try. So stop worrying about what others think, do, or say, and gain some distance. Then you can stand back with the angels and enjoy a sense of inner peace, knowing you do not need to take anything personally.

It's also important not to worry so much about loved ones. Remember, worry doesn't help our loved ones; they may even feel our worrying as a negative tug on their energy — the opposite effect from what we would want. The angels know when we are worrying out of love or out of a desire for power over others. They will transmit our messages as they see them coming from our heart; they will "call it like it is." If we attempt to have power over others or control their actions, our worry closes doors to others and comes back to us as more grief. If we send out the intention to love, the gates open wide, and when the energy comes back, we feel blessed.

There's no need to feel bad about worrying; it means that you care, but maybe too much. One fact of life is that we humans experience suffering. Another fact of life is that time heals, or makes whole again. If you make the choice not to fight these facts and you realize that the angels are willing to help, then you will find inner peace. So much good springs from inner peace; there is nothing better than a sense of mental, emotional, and physical ease. Whenever you begin to worry, get out into the open sea, where God and the angels can take care of you.

. . . .

PRACTICE IDEA: *Inner Peace*

Stop reading for a moment and think about any worries you may have. What are they? Where do you feel them in your body? Have they merely tormented your mind, or have they become a tense neck muscle, or a tight stomach? One way to release worry, or at least see it in a different light, is to converse with your guardian angel about your need to worry about something. Then let your guardian angel answer back with reasons why you would be better off releasing your worry and letting your angel take your problems to God for transmutation. Record your conversations and feelings on paper so you can review them in the future.

Prayer is another great way to release worry. When you pray, you engage the forces of change on a psychic level, and these forces will feed you solutions and positive messages and ideas for lightening up. Tune into the angelic consciousness and as soon as you find a worry, lighten up and let it go. Release all your worries to God and the angels, and they will be replaced with a renewed sense of self, hope, humor, and inner peace.

20

PATIENCE
INTO PEACE

Let nothing disturb you; nothing frighten you.
All things are passing.
God never changes.
Patience obtains all things.
Nothing is wanting to him who possesses God.
God alone suffices.

—ST. TERESA OF AVILA

THE OTHER DAY MY newspaper horoscope said, "With patience, you win." So I started thinking, where is the winning? How could patience give me the sense that I have won something? St. Teresa said, "Patience obtains all things." What she meant is that "in time" you have everything you need and will learn to want what you have. Yet if our time is spent suffering as the word *patient* connotes, then are we really winning? The magic behind patience is that when we practice patience, we back off from a situation and let time do us a favor; we "let go and let God." To make patience a divine experience, we need to be comfortable with giving up our need for control; we must have faith that there is a divine force of wisdom that can sort things out for us in beautiful ways we had not thought of.

Being patient reflects an inner conflict; if you have to exercise patience it means there is something stirring inside you to be impulsive, to express yourself, or to act out. To be *patient* means to bear affliction with calmness, and it comes from the Latin *pati,* which means suffer. To *be* a "patient," literally means to be someone who is suffering. "Patience is a virtue" goes the old saying. We have been beaten up a bit with the notion of virtue. Of course virtue is something to strive for, but in a natural way, and not by way of conforming to a rigid set of moral standards. Let's look beyond patience as a virtue. Too often this means we don't want to hear the still, small voice within. As I said before, we would not need patience if there wasn't something needing expression from a place deep within us.

When we are feeling impatient, we have to meet our impatience face-to-face, so that it won't develop into frustration. Often when we try to be patient, we fail. We are "trying" and not doing, and we are not paying attention to the inner messages the angels are sending us. What is our impatience wanting to tell us? When we find out, do we need to act on it? If so, what course of action would be best? Wisdom is our only tool in this regard. To get to the wisdom of a situation, it is helpful to take time out to meditate on the situation. Ask the angels to help position you for the best and highest outcome. The angels want us to reach for divine qualities on our own. They can hold the vision for us, but they can't do it for us. We must make the choice to change and go to new heights. As soon as we make this simple choice, they will be there to guide us.

. . . .

PRACTICE IDEA: *Patience*

To cultivate patience and calm, I highly recommend prayer. If you are suffering, if you feel your thoughts won't let you alone, begin to pray for guidance. Pretend you are a patient in the angels' hospital of love, and let them minister to you. The angels will guide you back to your center of love. Each time you feel yourself leaving this center, stop and pray again. Be childlike with your prayers; be spontaneous when you pray and never worry about using the right words. The angels and God listen to your heart, and they will answer your prayers "in time." Open your heart to their answers.

· 21 ·

WANTING WHAT
YOU HAVE

We are mortal, vulnerable, and fallible; our days
are numbered, often filled with sorrow, pain,
and humiliation. Some people think that this is a
good reason to avoid the here-and-now. I think that
this is a good reason to drink deep of the here-and-now.
—TIMOTHY MILLER, *How to Want What You Have*

T HE ANGELS HAVE UNIQUE and creative ways of getting
their messages to us, but we need to have an open
heart to hear and receive the subtle ones, which come to
us every day. Each day there will be at least one love
reminder sent to you from the angels. The reminders
may dawn on you later as something that you saw in the
sky or that you witnessed between two people. There are
so many ways to be reminded of love; all we need to do is
ask to be aware of these reminders, and our experience
of life will deepen, leading us into the realm of real
happiness.

Last night the television news was on while I was reading a magazine. I heard the newscaster talking about near-death experiences, and this grabbed my attention. A young boy, about twelve years old, had been near death in a coma when he awoke and started to talk to his father. His father told him that the doctors thought he shouldn't try to talk because it might be too much for his condition, but the boy said, "Dad, I have to tell you something. I met God." Of course his father had to listen. The boy said that God had told him one thing: "Don't take anything for granted." The boy is now in a wheelchair, and when he talked of this experience he was surrounded by an angelic aura, an inner glow of happiness that is unmistakably the angels' signature. This message is very simple, but very profound, especially coming from someone so young.

To take something for granted means not to appreciate it, to be so used to having something that we expect that it will always be there when we need it. Think of all the things we often take for granted: The sun coming up. The Earth giving us food. Our freedom. Our health. Our life. The list is endless. So many things that we take for granted could at any time change and be taken away from us. Then we might reevaluate our lives and realize that we could have lived just a little differently and fully appreciated the simple things in life.

Taking something for granted also means to assume without question. What do we go about assuming so often in our lives? We assume that our relationships will always be the way they are, but the nature of life is to change, so that assumption brings discord. We think that we must make assumptions, because after all we don't really know what someone else is thinking; we make our assumptions based on past experiences and think that our present assumption must be correct. This is an area for demonstrating great care. Assuming is not the same as having faith, although sometimes we confuse the two. Assumptions are human inventions, whereas faith is letting God and the angels know best. For deeper insight on the subject of assumptions, read *The Four Agreements: A Practical Guide to Personal Freedom* by don Miguel Ruiz.

Often we take it for granted that we are unhappy because we lack something. We think we must need more money, more things, more beauty, more love. By wanting more, we never spend our time enjoying and honoring what we have. While it is natural to want more out of life, that desire is fueled in unnatural ways in today's society. We are bombarded by messages all day long telling us we need more.

Consider for a moment what you really need more of. It won't be material things; you are probably doing just fine with what you have. The main thing you need is *less,* so you can enjoy what you *have* more. When you get to a point where you let go of the need for more, the angels will put you in line for a grant from Heaven. When you receive this grant, you will be blessed beyond compare by the simple things that surround you right now. Your grant from heaven will make it easier to catch the messages the angels continually transmit, and things will effortlessly come your way. It is your choice: You can give up wanting more, and be blessed with abundance, or you can fool yourself into thinking that getting more will fill the emptiness of what you believe you are missing in life.

We go to extremes with our need for material wealth. Financial wealth can certainly make some things easier, but material riches won't soothe your soul, or give you the inner peace you really need. If you have inner peace, then you have it all. Work on being rich in love. Pay attention to what this means to you and the ways in which you can really love. When you spend energy helping the angels, they will spend energy helping you, and you may find you are granted with "more" than you would ever think to ask for.

Think about the blessings you have been granted in life. Are you blessed with children, a home, a partner, or friends? In your mind make a list of the blessings life has granted you. What would your life be like if some of these gifts were taken away? Think about what you want to be granted; that is, what do you ask for over and over in your prayers? Now think about the things that we can never be granted, such as knowing when we, or others, will die; knowing what another person is thinking or will do; knowing anything certain about tomorrow. The most precious thing you have been given is this moment, right now.

. . . .

PRACTICE IDEA: *Inquire Within*

Whenever we are in the grips of wanting, it means there is something taking up a lot of our energy in the present for something that may or may not come in the future. We think if only I could get a better job, I would be happier and more successful. If only I had a good relationship, then I could do much more with my life. Holding your own particular want in mind, ask yourself the following questions.

Inquire Within

Do I really want this?

How do I know for certain?

Would having it change who I am?

Have I done anything to bring this into my life, or have I just complained or discussed my want at length?

Is wanting more comfortable to live with than having the actual experience?

Why don't I feel complete in being who I am right here, right now?

Am I really suffering without this want, or is the suffering based on something else?

How much time have I spent waiting for this?

Will having what I want really give meaning to my life, and how will I know?

What do I fear people will know about me if what I want doesn't come in time?

If the world was ending next week, would I still want this?

What would it be like to stop for a moment and want all that I have right now — to let go of the things I think I need?

Take a little vacation from wanting anything for the next twenty-four hours. You can ask the angels for help in this matter. Anytime you are taken out of the present, away from what you are doing by an urge of want, bring yourself back and think of something great about what you have. If the want won't go away, get up and go outside and consciously connect with something natural, like a tree, a flowering bush, the sky, or an animal. Breathe some fresh air. Take a drink of water. Warm yourself in the sun. Now, in this moment, is there anything else you need? Practice wanting what you have in this moment.

INDIGO IN THE NIGHT

*The quality, nature, and definition of
our thoughts determines the shape, clarity,
and color of our thoughtforms and of our auric field.
Raising our vibrations with sound and color —
the language of the angels.*

—TED ANDREWS

Y EARS AGO I WORKED at a camp in the mountains outside Los Angeles, where children from all walks of
"Angeleno" life would come and stay for two nights. The
camp was located in the mountains, which end on a beautiful stretch of rocky beach in Malibu. One of the activities for the two and a half days the children were with us
was a night hike. At the start of the hike we would tell the
children that they needed to use their night vision the way
nocturnal animals do. We told them it would take a little
getting used to because no flashlights would be allowed, .
and we were far away from city lights and street lights.

I'll never forget when some of the children would look up at the starry sky and ask, "What is all that stuff in the sky?" Many children had never seen more than one or two stars, and where we were you could see the Milky Way Galaxy on a good night. Another thing that struck me was the fact that a lot of these children just didn't go out at night in the inner cities; they stayed in and hoped that a stray bullet didn't sail through their window. Convincing the group that a night hike was a safe adventure to embark upon had to be handled very carefully. It included gaining a certain amount of trust since many of the children's experiences told them it was crazy to hike through the hills at night without flashlights.

Once we started out on the hiking trail and our eyes became used to the dark, we entered a magical world. One rule was no talking, because we needed to keep our senses alert and pay attention to the trail. We wouldn't want to miss the call of an owl, or if we were lucky, the sight of one. At one point on our hikes we always stopped in dark areas, where we would hand out Wintergreen mints and ask the children to pair off and watch each other bite into the mints to create the green sparks. In the clearing we would point out star constellations and maybe talk about the myths describing their origin. For me the night hikes were always special, especially when I had children in the group witnessing the natural world at night for the first time.

Each night hike was a unique experience because each night of the year is so different. Some nights we had no moon, and some nights the moon bathed us in bright silver light. Some nights were clear, and others misty, and of course the time of the year made a difference. But, most important, what evolved on our night hikes was a natural inclination to depend more on other senses than just our sense of sight. The children went into the unknown, with people they had only just met. They faced their fears and came back with priceless stories and a sense of accomplishment. When the hike was finished and the children were drinking their hot chocolate, the sense of aliveness and the exchange of stories in the room was amazing.

I am sad that this program no longer exists. The budget was cut because it was seen as superfluous. I am sad for the children who will never see the ocean and feel the sea breeze on their face. I cry for children who will never smell the rich scents of the forest while they still have the capacity for wonder. I am angry that most of the children in Los Angeles may never have the experience of feeling protected by a force only known in their heart, a force that one discovers from rich experiences in wild places.

❦

Each and every day, we receive the gifts of night, and yet sometimes we have no idea what these gifts are. The night is not our enemy. The night renews our spirit, refreshes our body, and makes us strong. Think of all the things we can experience at night. When we sleep we let ourselves go into the unknown, where we cannot control the images that come to us in dreams, where the possibility of a nightmare is ever-present. There are times you might stay awake on a vigil of worry or caretaking. When we emerge in the morning after all of this journeying we often find we have a new strength.

One of my friends, the artist Arthur Douët, reminds people to appreciate how magical and rich the nighttime is. He says he is often inspired to paint a background of the night in his paintings of angelic beings and divine energies. I love the way the night sky shows up in his paintings, and I asked Arthur about it. He replied, "Night has always been so beautiful for me, the softness of that indigo. I feel that it has always been just as sacred as the bright electrical light of the day." Arthur does paintings for many people of their angels or of a divine imprint of what is going on with them. He told me that more than once when he has painted someone's angel and put the night sky in the background, the person liked the angels but didn't like the dark night sky behind it. Most likely they were avoiding and fearing the dark nights we must go through at times.

It has been said that the angels do a lot of inner work with us when we sleep, at night when the sacred indigo surrounds us. We could make our sleep even more transforming if we became aware of this and made a point to remember our dreams and not to carry negative imagery with us into dreamtime. I discussed this in my first book, *Messengers of Light,* in which I shared a moment I had with my niece when she was about four years old. She had been staying up too late while I was baby-sitting, and one night, in another attempt to stay up late, she told me I shouldn't worry about when she went to sleep. She explained that when she slept, two angels flew around her all night, keeping away the monsters and ghosts so she could get a good night's sleep. My niece didn't know at the time that I was so keenly interested in angels, and what she said made sense to me. Just remember, the angels are always with you, and they spend a lot of time chasing our personal monsters and ghosts away.

. . . .

PRACTICE IDEA: *The Color Indigo*

Take some time to cultivate an appreciation for the night and for the color indigo. Ask the angels to help you. Watch the night sky on a clear night, visit an observatory, or go to a lecture on astronomy. Think about the aurora borealis, comets, and the silvery moonlight we only see at night, beautiful against the darkness. Think about the quiet at midnight, the stillness, the blackness, and the peace just before dawn. Then take a moment to express your gratitude for the gifts of the night.

· 23 ·

EMBRACING

THE SHADOW

One does not become enlightened
by imagining figures of light but
by making the darkness conscious.
—C. G. JUNG

T HE ABOVE QUOTE IS seen often these days, because it makes an important point for anyone who is sincerely seeking enlightenment. We live in a physical world of polar opposites; when we deny the realities of our world and its Spiritual Law, we miss enlightenment. It is important to note that as humans we embody both the qualities of the divine and the shadow side of these qualities. Angels live in the light. Humans live with the light inside them, but we also live in the world of day and night, light and dark, yin and yang. Some people who realize the goodness of angels get so carried away with the angelic force that they expect to behave just like angels. That is why it is especially important that we "make the darkness conscious" because when we make the decision to bring qualities of the Divine into our consciousness and to practice loving God, the opposite qualities often crop up and demand attention.

The shadow opposes the ideals of the ego, and if we load our boat with too much of the light and forget to acknowledge the shadow, the shadow side will sink the boat. Often when discussing the shadow, a sense of seriousness surfaces almost immediately. Yet, a shadow is simply a normal side effect of standing in the light. We can't afford to pretend that the shadow leaves us when we find the angels; we are still in a human body that reflects light and casts a shadow. Just as the beautiful night sky shows us the stars, planets, and other wonders that we cannot see in the day, our shadow asks us to acknowledge more than the comfortable, ordered, divine, or sterile aspects of life.

People often fail to acknowledge the dark urges and inferior qualities demanding attention from the unconscious shadowy realm of their psyches. Waiting in the shadows, left to their own devices, these characteristics gather energy and force their way out. "The devil made us" commit adultery, injure someone in a fistfight, or steal money from elders on tight pensions. It could very well be that "the devil made us do it," at least metaphorically, so now what? How do we get to the point where "the devil is making us do something"? This happens when we don't acknowledge the coexistence of dark and light, and when we project the darkness that is within us out onto someone else, or onto the proverbial evil *them*.

Why do so many people believe that darkness is bad, even on par with the word *evil*? If darkness were simply bad and lightness simply good, the world would be easily understood. This is just not the case. Good and bad, right and wrong, are human judgments and projections onto things in life that we often don't fully understand. As we know, when we judge, we put ourselves on a level of higher authority where we have no business being. What we observe and then judge is a matter of personal perception, projection, and programmed behavior.

One of Aesop's fables tells of a woman, moved by compassion one winter's day, who brings a frozen snake into her house and warms it with her kindness. She "holds it to her bosom," and then the snake, thawed enough so its natural instinct has returned, gives her a fatal bite. She says, "How could you repay me this way when I showed you such kindness?" And, the snake says, "Silly woman, what did you expect? I am a snake."

Human nature covers the entire map, and you may find yourself in unfriendly territory at times. There are many people who compulsively look for those with a sincere desire to heal and help so that they can take advantage of what is offered. Many victims are created when compassionate humans with good intentions get involved with psychopaths, the most unnatural of humans. There is a big difference between being naive and being innocent. Does it help to believe that humans are basically good at heart? It depends on whether you think all Homo sapiens are actually human. Animals oftentimes treat us better than other humans. So stay as awake and conscious as you can.

If you are afraid of your shadow, then practice the quality of humility. Whenever excessive pride is present in our consciousness, it is as if we have placed a personal call to the trickster archetype, and invited this energy to its favorite type of party. The devil has no choice but to ignore a humble soul, because humility allows humans to admit our faults in the light of God's love, and to deal with our dark thoughts and anger without violence. Those who are truly humble can laugh at themselves in a divine way. When we display a sense of humility, the negative pole of darkness has not been served; the light has been honored and made stronger.

Chasing money is another area in which the shadow can be observed. While money itself is simply energy that can be used for a full range of purposes, pursuing money at the expense of other qualities and values creates a void which can never be filled. When we get caught in this cycle, it seems that there will never be enough. Groveling and scheming for money is boring and uncreative. What *is* interesting is when people stop groveling for money, when they stop compromising their values and their families, and come back to the realization that money can only offer a temporary high, and not a very good one at that. Learning to live more simply, and being grateful for what we have, brings us into closer alignment with the great Law.

Once we integrate the shadow side of money — once we come out of our denial and recognize it for the neutral energy that it is — we can begin to live our lives in true abundance. This includes full expression of the natural tendency to share our abundance with others. It is also important to note that people have different life paths concerning money. It is definitely possible to accumulate great wealth and follow a spiritual path, but because of our society's obsession with material accumulation, this path poses some additional challenges. Again, the angels can help us stay honest with ourselves as we find the path that is most appropriate for us.

. . . .

PRACTICE IDEA: *Embracing the Shadow*

Consider spending one day looking at the way the shadow manifests in your life. You might want to note what you discover about yourself in this process. What are the things you avoid acknowledging about yourself? How can you learn from them? Remember, it is possible — and indeed advisable — to engage in this process with a sense of humor rather than moral judgment. Facing the shadow with full awareness will make you stronger and better equipped to join with the angels in all areas of your life. So, you have weaknesses. So, you are not perfect. *So what!* What is so bad about that? Your imperfections are your beauty marks. If you are sincere about knowing the Divine, you cannot deny the shadow aspects of being human. Practice true humility and accept yourself as you are. The angels will give you all the support you need.

24

THE RAINBOW
COVENANT

As is the human body,
so is the cosmic body.
As is the microcosm,
so is the macrocosm.
As is the atom,
so is the universe.
—THE UPANISHADS

TAKE A MOMENT AND try to remember the most beautiful rainbow you ever witnessed, or close your eyes and imagine a perfect rainbow arching across a rain-soaked vista. Now think of what the rainbow symbolizes to you personally. Rainbows remind us that sunlight actually consists of a spectrum of color. Rainbows come at the edge of rainstorms, when the sun breaks through even though it may still be raining. So a rainbow symbolizes hope, because even though there is rain —which is often said to stand for the emotions — the beautiful possibilities begin to shine through with the sun. Dream dictionaries often state that dreaming of a rainbow means a time of great blessings, or a time to celebrate the end of despair. In many cultures a rainbow symbolizes the bridge between Heaven and Earth. In the Old Testament, a rainbow appeared to Noah after the floodwaters had receded as a symbol of God's favor and sacred covenant with humanity.

We live in a world of changing seasons, day and night, moon and sun, ebb tides and flood tides, yet most days we don't even give one thought to the rhythms of Mother Earth. Homes and offices are designed to keep the elements out. Some people leave the building where they live by walking into the garage, getting into their cars, driving to work, and getting out in another garage, which leads them into their office where they spend all day working. Unless they go outside to get their paper in the morning or lunch in the afternoon, they spend entire days not even knowing what the air feels or smells like that day, or how warm the sun is. If we don't get outside once in a while or pay attention to what is going on in nature around us, we miss an integral part of our connection with the angels.

The human experience has become distorted because we are so out of touch with what is natural. Professor and writer Gregory Bateson stated, "The major problems in the world are the result of the differences between the way nature works and the way man thinks."

Perhaps if we looked into the ecological problems afflict-
ing the Earth, and found the people responsible for decisions that lead to the affliction, we might find that these
people have no *reverent* connection with the element that
they are polluting. Sometimes they do have a connection,
but it is cast aside and forgotten when the time comes to
make a decision about dumping chemicals in the ocean on
Monday, after they spent Sunday deep-sea fishing.

Many crucial decisions made about Mother Earth
are made in penthouse office suites, with controlled air, fake
plants, and no water in sight, as far away from the soil of the
Earth as one can get in everyday life. All around the world,
financially powerful people in penthouse office suites in
skyscrapers are making crucial decisions about forests and
wetlands without any connection to them; they are as far
away from the ground as they can get, except in air travel.

Our bodies are made of the same materials that are
found naturally in the Earth. We spend time on the Earth
each day, but some days are spent virtually *out of touch*
with the Earth that is living, breathing, and alive with
spirit. Whole days are spent not touching a tree, or being
blessed by the fragrance of a flower, or watching the sky
for the angels' cloud art.

Some people think that the Earth has evil energy
— that when an earthquake or hurricane occurs, it is

intrinsically bad. One of the most inane things happening on television news shows are the titles that they give to nature's events. Each station comes up with a creative title for natural events, and some even have little theme songs to go along with the drama. Right now in California heavy rains are causing terrible damage to property; the newscasters have dubbed this "Nature's Wrath."

Why would rain be a personal attack of rage and vengeance on us poor little humans who choose to live in flood plains, on the ever-changing landscape of hillsides, and in expensive homes built at the mighty ocean's edge? Nature is not on a personal vendetta against us. We need to quit fighting nature and trying to tame or control it. Some of the problems humans face during disasters can be traced to greed and arrogance; others are simply the way things happen sometimes.

God has never said that the Earth and its natural ways are evil. To separate, and to slander or lie, is the original meaning of the word *evil*. What brings us most of our problems is the illusion of separation from nature and the rest of humanity. When we separate ourselves from the Earth by thinking that it is a big inanimate object to pillage and tame, we lack a reverence for life, and we ignore one of the best ways to achieve divinity: the beauty of nature. When we separate ourselves from what we know is right and true, and seek what is false and illusory, we create an imbalance in ourselves. Then our actions, thoughts, and intentions are dis-integrated and the ills of racism, wars, injustice, and hatred are the result. When we separate ourselves from God and the angels, we separate ourselves from the light, and live in the darkness.

. . . .

PRACTICE IDEA: *What is Sacred?*

Take a moment to consider what is sacred to you. I love trees, and often I have a direct experience of the Divine when I connect with a tree and its guardian spirit. When I write I always make sure there is a tree I can look upon out my window; I stop and focus on the tree when I need to be refreshed. My intention is to have reverence; by being aware of trees on a deeper level, my soul takes in a mighty form of beauty like no other. Think of a way you can connect with nature in a sacred way, and practice it daily. If you have a tree you love, make greeting it the first thing you do in the morning. You might also choose to greet the sun as an uplifting way to start your day in tune with the angels.

25

Natural Colors
Don't Clash

*The resurgence of the real poses challenges
and opportunities that we are only beginning to grasp.
A wise response must be based on an understanding
of how and why the modern assumptions arose,
often for fully admirable reasons. How did we ever
come to perceive body and mind as separate,
nature as dead resource, and place as inconsequential?*
—CHARLENE SPRETNAK, *A Resurgence of the Real*

L ATELY I HEAR A lot of talk about what the writer
Charlene Spretnak calls "the real" in book titles, magazine articles, and everyday conversations. I hear myself
using the word often; I find myself wanting to talk about
real life, real connections, real money, and real time. This
is because life today does not seem real to me. Money has
lost a sense of reality for most of the population because
of credit cards, debit cards, and checking accounts. Real
connections with other humans seem to be more difficult.
Most friendships are kept alive through telephone connections. Time seems to be less real than it used to be.

Many people agree on the idea that things are speeding up, and this gives us the feeling we have less real time.

The good news is that if we really want to be real, we don't have to go past our own backyard, or acquire more money and time; we simply need to reconnect with the elements of the natural world. The key is not just to talk about it, but to *experience* the elements in our own unique ways. When the unreal seems to be taking over, I know that in order for me to feel real and centered, I need to get out into the natural world and converse with the elements, the nature spirits, and the earth angels.

Imagine taking a walk in a garden filled with every flower ever designed by the angels. Gather a bouquet of flowers, making sure to pick a variety of colors. Now hold your bouquet in front of you and try to find some colors or flowers that clash or feel discordant. There may be some that you enjoy more than others, but if you free your mind to just be with the flowers, you will find that all the colors belong; they are perfect in being what they are. Now imagine a bowl of fruit. Again, is there any need to redesign for color coordination? Listen to the songbirds. Are they singing off-key?

Now imagine a group of humans in a crowded bank on a Friday afternoon. Many people would look around and start to criticize others: "Gee, that lady shouldn't be wearing that outfit. . . . Oh, that person could use a nose job. . . . Oh, that person had a bad nose job." I often hear people discuss the new people they are dating by describing little details of their face, hands, hair style, or lack of hair. Quite often I have heard people say they just can't go out with certain people again because their flawed looks bother them, or they can't stand the color of their hair, or the way their arms seem too short. Is this what we want to focus on? How did all of this extreme criticism about our bodies get to be so prevalent? What makes people focus on perceived imperfections in the human body? Can we change this?

With all the images of idealized beauty we are bombarded with in this worldly society, criticism is encouraged on a regular basis. While it's natural that certain things attract us, and we each have our own way of perceiving beauty, I believe that much of our unhappiness comes from failing to recognize the light and beauty that is within our fellow life forms. God is present everywhere, in each face that reflects the light. When you learn to cultivate this view, you will see what the angels see.

I think that it is interesting that we don't hear much criticism about the way babies and small children look physically. When I look at a baby, I see a new form of God. Can you imagine looking at a newborn spark of God and saying,

"I think we need to change its mouth, and those little hands are too pudgy; maybe it should be put on a diet." When I do hear an adult discussing the "good looks" of particular children or comparing them to their playmates in degrees of "prettiness," I get a sense that something is not right. This kind of talk sounds like fingernails on a chalkboard to me. For many years I worked with children of all ages, and they all looked beautiful to me. One of the saddest transitions I noticed is that as they matured, they began to find all kinds of things that seemed imperfect in themselves.

. . . .

PRACTICE IDEA: *Inner Light*

God and the angels don't judge our looks; the nature spirits don't deny us the beauty of nature based on physical appearance. The etheric realm recognizes us by our inner light. I believe that if humans could practice more light recognition among one another, the rate of happiness would increase tremendously. Practice recognizing the light in all life forms. Ask the angels and God to help you see as they see. Soon this will become a joyful part of your approach to life. Take a look around and start to see the light.

26

THE FIVE
ELEMENTS

The moment one gives close attention to anything,
even a blade of grass, it becomes a mysterious,
awesome, indescribably magnificent world in itself.
—HENRY MILLER

THE FIVE ELEMENTS — fire, water, air, earth, and ether — form the basis for ancient ways of knowing and attempting to explain the physical world. We have an ancient memory of how important these elements are for understanding life. The elements share a form of consciousness much like a very impersonal angelic force that keeps things going at the primal level of creation. If we become more aware of, intimate with, and most important reverent of these five elements, our lives open up to new blessings, creativity, and a deeper connection with the angels.

Within us there is a guiding impulse to restore our true nature, or our sense of health and wholeness with each of the five elements:

Fire. This element represents the spirit. Sight is the sense corresponding to fire and spirit. Through our spirit, we meet the angels of fire; divine vision and insight are ways to strengthen our spirit.

Water. This element represents the soul; our soul is the realm of our spiritual treasures. The sense of taste comes into play for soul and water. The soul holds the impulse to taste and savor the flavors of life in a deeper more mysterious way, in which explanation and logic stay outside the gate.

Air. Our mind corresponds with the element of air. The sense corresponding to mind is touch, so we call upon the aspects of touch, to get in touch, to link up with the angels. To understand our mind and the qualities of inspiration (the breath of God), we meet the angels of air.

Earth. This element represents our physical body, which is made up of the same minerals and chemicals found throughout the planet we live on. Our sense of smell brings us closer to the angels of the Earth. It never lies to us; the angels of the Earth help us to know what is real and to honor physical matter. Angels leave wonderful heavenly scents when they have been "physically" near.

Ether. Our heart is our guide into the higher realms of ether. The elemental influences are all equal in importance, but ether, the fifth element, is the one that pervades all the others. We may know it as chi or qi energy, prana, life force, or God energy. Looking at the importance of sound and vibration will allow us a deeper understanding of ether. Just as ether pervades and gives energy to all other elements, our heart is the center of energy in our bodies that gives life to all our other organs. It is also the center where we truly meet God. When you follow your heart, you find your own way home.

The angels guide us to practice poise in the five domains, or fields of consciousness, in which we experience the world: in our will to act (spirit or fire), poise in our feeling (soul or water), in our thinking (mind or air), in our temple (body or earth), and in our divine connection (heart or ether). There is an instinctive agreement in the human psyche about these five integral domains that work in their own ways to bring us the human experience through this divine composition.

One way of imagining this is: First, we are spirit; we agree on a soul — a calling for our spirit. Then we merge with air and take our first breath, which begins our physical presence on Mother Earth. Ether keeps us going, ensuring that the elements vibrate in a certain pattern so that we can be who we are and have a spiritual experience on Earth while sharing our own special gift of love from our heart.

❦

The five elements are circular in nature. Water creates a circle when we drop something into it, and it forms a spiral when it drains. Fire burns in a circle, and we are inclined to create a circle around a fire. Air whirls into a circle at times, and we often say, "Let the air circulate." The Earth is a circle, and ether encircles all of it. The word *enchantment* means to encircle with song, which is the role of ether, the primal sound.

Wheels represent cycles and rhythms, another thing humans cannot afford to ignore. The wheel, or mandala, is a sacred magic circle. Psychologist Carl Jung encouraged the use of mandalas as a contemplation tool to understand that life has meaning and order, and that this knowledge can bring us inner peace. He believed that constructing mandalas could lead to inner balance and understanding.

We also find inner balance and inner peace by spending time in the mysterious unseen world of the nature devas and amusing nature spirits. Have you ever felt restored after sitting by a quiet lake, soaking away your troubles in a hot bath, or being rocked by the waves of the ocean? Have you ever felt as if all you needed was a deep breath of fresh air, or a visit from a cool breeze, and you would be centered and renewed? Have you ever felt the impulse to walk barefoot on the Earth, lie down and daydream on a grassy knoll, or hug a warm boulder to feel grounded? Have you ever marveled at the significance of the hearth or home fire, or lighted a candle and felt the special peace it conveys? Have you witnessed a glimpse of the etheric realm? Have you ever been touched by the divine love of the angels, or been infused with love and happiness for no reason?

If you answered yes to any of these questions, then you have been intimate with the elements and allowed their energy to heal you. If you answered yes and your experience made you feel closer to God and more whole and centered, then you have been divinely intimate with the angels of nature.

. . . .

PRACTICE IDEA: *Enjoying the Elements*

We live in an enchanted world with angels singing to us. Opening our senses up to the Divine and enjoying a mystical intimacy with the elements, is within reach of everyone. This happens naturally when you let the angels orchestrate the balance of elements in your life. But if you are out of touch with a particular element, then you most likely "feel out of touch" with a part of yourself. Get back in touch by enjoying a physical experience with each of the five elements. This will have a profound healing effect upon you, especially if you do it while paying attention to the angels.

Practice some breathing exercises, or simply take notice of the air you are breathing in and out. Light a candle and enjoy its beauty. Walk barefoot on the earth; touch the soil with your hands. Bathing in water definitely seems to be able to reach the soul and soothe it. Follow the angels' encouragement and get out into nature more often. You can gain insight into your particular needs by noticing what you are attracted to, what your interests are, or what your yearnings are. Also, sometimes the most crucial breath of air, the most thirst quenching drink of water, or the most intense spark of fire or passion is experienced in the realm of the psyche, where it is reached through a dream or insight, instead of a physical experience.

27

ELEMENTAL
ESSENCE

The Buddha stays on Yon San Mountain,
picking up flowers, transmitting Dharma.
Cool Wind. Flower and Moon.
Each thing is complete.

—ANONYMOUS

I HAVE NOTICED IN myself and the people I know well that we all seem a little out of touch with one of the five elements and very connected with at least one of the others. Sometimes, without stretching the imagination, I can correlate this to a person's astrological chart. For example, I feel as if I was born with a built-in understanding of fire. I am not claiming to know everything about fire, but something in my psyche feels a level of intimacy with fire.

One summer when I was around ten, my neighborhood friend and I devoted any time we could to "playing with matches" and experimenting with fire. Both of us have several fire signs prominent in our astrological charts. Some of our little fires bordered on dangerous, and we are very lucky no real damage was done, thanks to the angels, no doubt. I would *never* recommend this to anyone, yet I have to say I learned a lot that summer about the intrinsic nature of fire, and I developed a healthy reverence for it.

Air, especially wind, I do not have such intimacy with. I feel very uncomfortable in dry air and have never fully appreciated air-conditioning. I feel instantly "out of my element" when the famous Santa Ana winds blow through Southern California. I have lived where the threat of losing my house to a brush fire fanned by the "devil winds" has come way too close more than once. So my experiences of wind have not helped, and have left imprints of fear. I have a friend who loves the wind, and is an air sign astrologically. This friend, who is highly intelligent, has no clue how to make a good fire. Even candles burning seem to throw this person off. One time, a fire this friend had built in a fireplace went completely out of control, and I instinctively knew what to do to contain it. This same person is in tune with air, and is very sensitive to air quality. Not to stereotype, but many of my friends past and present who are air signs have an issue with the properties of fire, and, as we know, air can make fire burn out of control.

This is not a book on astrology, and I am certainly not an astrologer, but I want to point out that the elements comprise a big part of the mythic influence and the energy patterns of astrology. One way we can learn to gain more insight on the elements missing or weak in our lives is by looking at our astrological chart. Astrology does not provide the whole picture of a person, and astrology is not exact — as I mentioned before, I think that it is lacking in the area of the divine feminine — but it can offer some interesting dimensions to explore.

If we form an appreciation for all the elements and get to know how to use the ones we feel out of touch with, then we will naturally feel more balanced and have a well-rounded reverence for life. One theory says that the element we are least familiar with holds magic for us, when we dare to integrate its qualities into our life. Often we project our missing elements onto others before we are willing to own them. For instance, think of someone you admire but feel different from, and figure out what element that person holds that you don't. Within this element is a key to some potential that you have inside yourself; if you explore the missing element, it could provide one of the keys to your calling.

. . . .

PRACTICE IDEA: *Understanding Your Element*

In our quest to understand ourselves, we often focus too much on what is seen, known, and comfortable. Most interesting to me is the idea that it is important not to overdevelop and focus on what is obvious and easy for us to grasp, but rather to investigate what is mysterious to us and feels alien to our elemental makeup. Carl Jung called this "the inferior function." According to Jung, it can be very beneficial to meet the lesser known aspects of ourselves. So, once again, the element we least embody or express provides us with the best access to our magic, the place where the angels enter boldly.

Try exploring the theory that whatever element feels the least familiar may be a way to access tremendous creative fire and generate inspiration for your life. What heals you may entail going back to what made you ill. Your weakness can become your biggest strength, just as the most brittle bone when broken heals to be stronger than the rest. Consider exploring these ideas in whatever way feels good to you.

· 28 ·

PRECIOUS FLUID
OF HEAVEN

*The sense of rhythm is ancient. All life came out of
the ocean; each one of us comes out of the waters of
the womb; the ebb and flow of the tides is alive in the
ebb and flow of our breathing. When you are in rhythm
with your nature, nothing destructive can touch you.
Providence is at one with you; it minds you and brings you
to your new horizons. To be spiritual is to be in rhythm.*

—JOHN O'DONOHUE, *Anam Cara*

ANCIENT PHILOSOPHERS CONSIDERED WATER the first
element, the mother of all things. Water is a symbol
of life, because without it there is no life as we know it.
The baptismal font was once designed as a womb — the
womb of Mary, the divine feminine — and baptism was a
birth to spirit or fire. The symbolic act of baptism
includes many things, one of which is the bringing of
Heaven to Earth and humanity to the heavens. Water is
used for cleansing, and holy fire — representing the holy
spirit — is the means by which we are purified. Water
flows downward and fire flames upward; then a new

breath is taken as an initiation into the air element and the ethers.

Certain mystery school teachings say that the ceremony of baptism was originally a near-death experience in which initiates were held under water until they actually began to drown, after which they would be revived. The idea of rebirth became more than an abstract concept; it was an actual event, which had powerful repercussions on each person's psyche. The fact that the baptismal font was described as a womb reinforces this idea of being born again, to the life of the soul rather than the body.

The goddess religions almost always created shrines to the feminine near wells, lakes, springs, or seas. Grottos dedicated to Mary often have a blessed spring of water emerging. Water is maternal. The Lady of the Lake is the goddess of love, and water is often used in metaphors for love. We are starved for a mythic connection to life, and nothing speaks more of our mythic starvation than the worldwide response to the death of Princess Diana, who is now a Lady of the Lake.

Various mythologies allude to water as the precious fluid of Heaven. The Chinese referred to the moon as the "pot" that held the water that was the source of life on Earth, while the Egyptians believed that tears from the eyes of the Mother Goddess produced life-giving rain.

Should the goddess go on a crying jag, however, flooding was the unfortunate result. In addition, every culture has a belief in the Well of Life, the Water of Life, or the Fountain of Youth.

Water of the ocean represents the unconscious, the inner depths, the realm of the soul. This is the world of feelings, of intuition, of spiritual yearnings — the real location of the mythological wellsprings of youth and immortality. When we listen to our feelings, when we acknowledge our deepest desires, when we search for soulful as well as physical equilibrium, we become connected to the divine wisdom that is the source of eternal life. We become happier and more fulfilled, and, in the process, more youthful and energized.

Age and death cease to have meaning when we are so connected to the passions of our soul that we have no time to be consumed with anything but the sheer joy of existence. By the same token, when we ignore our feelings and our soul's needs, our lives become empty, dry, and desolate. We may experience anxiety or nightmares, as our unheard selves squirm in the depths of our unconscious like the mythological dragons and serpents lurking beneath the surface of the sea, demanding to be confronted and tamed before the gateway to paradise can be flung open.

One afternoon I was visiting my friend Jai during a heat wave. It was so hot and dry outside that we felt wilted and lifeless. Inside, the air-conditioning didn't seem to be making much of a difference, and we started discussing how disconnected from life we felt. The more we discussed how arid we felt, the more hopeless we became. We got to the point where we felt the hot, dry air was signaling the end of the world. After we went on with our drama for a while, I said to Jai, "We need water. Not a drink of water — much more than that; we need to water our beings." So I suggested that we call in the angels of water by going outside and making it rain.

Outside Jai's house is a lovely flagstone patio, with beautiful trees, plants, and even a fountain surrounded by ferns, yet everything looked the way we felt: parched, dry, and arid. We each grabbed a hose and started spraying water on everything, all over each other and the fountain, the ferns, and the trees. Pretty soon we were laughing and joyous, and a little bird started to frolic in the water and sing to us. We felt restored by the water experience, and the garden seemed happy and so much greener. A friend stopped by to visit and we told her that it had just rained, only on us in this little area. The trees were still dripping water and she started to believe us, and we told her it was like a miracle. Then we told her what had really happened, and she loved it. We all laughed and talked about how miraculous water really is, and how it healed our lack of life force.

Many times I have experienced the feeling of needing a shower, swim, or bath to get centered after experiencing a difficult situation. One time a window fell on my hand and badly broke two of my fingers. The moment after this happened, I got in the shower and let the flowing water wash away the shock. Then I felt more centered and figured out what to do next. I feel claustrophobic if I don't have good water to drink, or access to a shower. My point is that water, besides being very important to our basic physical survival, is also very important to our psychic and soul survival.

I wonder if the increased appreciation for the idea of soul in the last few years, which is often talked of in terms of water, has stimulated our desire for more fountains in our lives. It is interesting to me that table fountains are so popular, along with fountains for the garden, which used to be difficult to find and extremely expensive, but are now an integral part of each garden center. Many people don't go anywhere without a bottle of water in their hands, and for some people their water bottle seems almost like a security blanket. Perhaps they are protecting their soul with this symbolic act. Water is also symbolic of our connection to the feminine. By having a reverence for water, we are helping to bring in the dimensions of the divine feminine so needed in our world today.

. . . .

PRACTICE IDEA: *Water Yourself*

Consider the importance of water in nurturing your being. What aspect of life for you is most like the water — deep and mysterious? What seems to nurture, cleanse, and give you life? What aspect of your life might need cleansing, rebirth, new insight, and a renewed attitude?

Close your eyes now, and let the message or image of water be absorbed into your unconscious, planting itself as a seed of new awareness and growth. Think about the many forms water can take, and the images of water that speak most strongly to you. Water may stand still, in a pool or pond, reflecting something important in your life. It may come to you as a river, the life source of entire civilizations. You may see it as a stream, and perhaps you will feel the need to think about things in stream-of-consciousness fashion. Water may flow from a well, which provides you with sustenance, nourishment, and insight. It may come in the form of a cloud or mist; the Chinese believed that clouds were formed in the union of yin and yang, symbolizing peace. If something was shrouded in mist, it had a mysterious or magical meaning. Play with the many forms that water can take, and drink deeply to quench your thirst.

· 29 ·

Inspiration in
the Air

The world of thought resides in the air.
All of our thoughts happen in the air element.
Our greatest thoughts come to us from
the generosity of the air. It is here that the
idea of inspiration is rooted — you inspire or
breathe in the thought concealed in the air element.

—JOHN O'DONOHUE

AIR IS THE LINK between Earth and Heaven, our physical and spiritual selves. We sometimes hold the idea
that air is empty and idle, since it is something that we
don't see in the same way that we see a fire burn, or water
fall. Take a moment and think about all the things happening in the air right now. How does it feel: warm, cool,
damp, dry? What does it smell like? If you are inside a
dwelling, think about the difference in the air outside.
Think about all the signals passing through the air right
now. Think about where the angels are. When my friend
Shannon's son Gideon was around six, we asked him what

he thought angels were. He answered, "Oh, they are just plain old air."

We experience air in continually changing ways. It may be still and calm, or heavy with impending rain. It may be warm with the comfort of the summer, or chilly with the breath of winter. It may come with the sweet touch of a gentle breeze or the fury of a tornado. It may carry us along on a strong current, within which there may be other winds, forces of energy, and change blowing simultaneously. It may take part of us here and part of us there, or mask inner movement with an outward appearance of stillness.

With breath and air we are introduced to many fragrances and smells each day. Our sense of smell is one of our most powerful senses, and most reliable in terms of memory. A smell in the air can instantly trigger a memory from long ago in our childhood. I once had a teacher who recommended that if we were at a party and interested in meeting someone to date, instead of going by sight we should trust our sense of smell. By doing this we would end up with a deeper connection and a better match of chemistry between us.

Honor your sense of smell. I think it will become even more important to us in the future, as we have to rely more and more on the unseen. There are many things in the air today that we must admit just don't belong there — including the chemical pollutants our cars and factories spew out. Since air is mostly invisible to our sight, it is important that we have faith in the air as well as our sense of smell.

<hr/>

The air is the realm of ideas, and air reminds us of the power of inspiration. As thought always precedes action, so success in any endeavor must be built on a firm strategic foundation, and must have divine inspiration to energize it. Inspiration is the breath of God; it is the divine life force that keeps us vital. The best thing about inspiration is that it is free. You cannot actually buy it, even though it may come from something you bought. Inspiration exists within and around you at all times; your job is to keep your inspiration receptor sites wide open to receiving.

Too much inner talk and explanation can drive away the special energy and gift of inspiration. For example, say you read a beautiful story of someone who witnessed a true miracle from Heaven, and it leaves your skin tingling and a feeling of hope in your heart. Now what do you think happens when you start thinking too much about it and asking questions that only God can answer? Such questions might include: "How do we know that this really happened, and that the person isn't just making up a story? Why did the angels guide this person out of sickness or danger, and let others suffer or die in similar instances?" These questions tend to dampen our enthusiasm. Inspiration is a gift to the mind, yet the mind can easily block it or ruin it.

I have noticed over the years that some writers and scholars who want to be known for their intellect, get technical over such questions as whether or not angels have wings. In fact, I have read recently published books that seem to want to wipe out popular conceptions of angels, and replace beautiful imaginings with something very dull. I wonder where these writers and scholars are getting their information. Is it from deep knowing and experience? Where is the inspiration?

As humans we respond to symbols. We express divine beauty and insight in our art. If there is a preponderance of art depicting angels with wings, obviously this symbolizes something real within the collective psyche. Angels appear to humans according to human capacity to accept and understand the appearance. Wings are symbolic of a divine connection with beauty, so let it be. Since when did arguing over the particulars of angels, such as how many can dance on the head of a pin, ever give us anything short of a headache. The angels inspire, and that is what is left in our heart after an angel experience.

. . . .

PRACTICE IDEA: *Inspiration*

Start the process of inspiration by taking a deep breath. Inhale deeply while imagining that you are breathing in the love and inspiration of the angels. Then let your breath go in a long exhalation. Each breath can become an opportunity to air out your mind and rediscover the source of your deepest inspiration. By cultivating the quality of inspiration, you open new vistas that lead to creative thinking and a fuller, more joyful expression of love.

· 30 ·

Let Your Mind
Sit on Your Heart

Bad, good, different, same, up, down — all exist in
the mind, not the heart. . . . And if the mind sits on
the heart, then it will have a nice perspective. If not,
it just chases its own tail until it's kissed by an angel,
the kiss of peace, and then it will never be the same.
The heart will expand and explode with joy, paling the
mind to insignificance in the volcano of fire and life.
—RICHARD STINE

I LOVE THIS WRITING by Richard Stine for many reasons.
I think that it brings up some powerful truths about
the heart and why we have so much trouble following
our heart — at least until the angels come around
with "the kiss of peace." Once this happens, it is true, we
are never the same. When the angels touch us, we are
never able to ignore our heart, because we have given it a
chance to open and to love. Now we have a problem of
sorts, because our heart will want more chances to
love, and it doesn't worry about breaking or the pain
involved when we suffer loss. The heart has courage and

knows that no matter what, love is worth every moment of pain.

The heart is a mysterious organ. It continues to mystify medical scientists; discoveries about how the electromagnetic field of the heart responds to emotional stimulus are giving us insight into how important love and relationships are to the health of the heart and the body. The heart is natural; it is uncorrupted, untouched, and free to follow its course. The natural course for the heart is to love, openly and freely. We like to hear that someone has a big heart. A big heart provides plenty of room for acceptance.

The heart is also wild. By understanding our own innate wildness, we learn to live in the heartland and know our heart-self. Sometimes we make fun of people who "live in their heart." Yet we must come to honor the parts of us that are heartfelt. When feelings come from our heart, we don't need to argue with them, intellectualize them, or analyze them. Our heart offers a connecting point for our relationship with God. Our heart is the home of our true intentions, and this is what God and the angels respond to. If your "heart is in the right place," God knows right where you are.

When you allow your life to be directed from within by your heart, you will know that the more you follow your heart — for answers, for making things happen, for finding your own way to the source of all love, and for living your life by your own choices — the happier and more successful you will be. Living from your heart and accepting personal responsibility for the bulk of what goes on in your life will give you the ingredients to truly connect with other people in healthy and special ways. A quote comes to mind from Antoine de Saint-Exupéry: "It is only with the heart that one can see rightly; what is essential is invisible to the eye." Follow your heart, and it will lead you away from fear, and into the bliss of deep love.

. . . .

PRACTICE IDEA: *Follow Your Heart*

Think of your heart as a messenger. What message does it have for you? Practice paying close attention to the messages of your heart each and every day. Notice how your joy and inner peace increases as you follow the guidance of your heart. Now think of your heart beating at the center of your body. Start breathing slowly and deeply, and imagine peace surrounding your heart with shimmering flecks of angelic light. Let the light flow into your blood-stream and bring peace to all your living cells. You may want to repeat this experience several times during the course of your day.

· 31 ·

THE GLOW
OF ANGELS

If we were to give up the "self project" so dear
to many therapies and theories of psychology,
education, and spirituality, we might see angels
once again; for the blazing light of self-interest
blanks out the glow of angels. . . . Whether we're
concerned about our own "self" or the "self" of others,
that attention blocks our appreciation of the angel who
stands at the doorway of the truly deep and intimate.
—THOMAS MOORE, *The Re-Enchantment of Everyday Life*

THE ABOVE QUOTATION FROM writer Thomas Moore
reminds me that we need the sacred fire within us to
be bright, but not overpowering. If our fire, our spirit, is
blazing with too much self-interest, then we block out the
glow of the angels. If our spirit is a beautiful flame that
glows like a candle and radiates love, then we will be in
the right light to see the glow of the angels.

Of all the elements, fire is perhaps most directly
symbolic of the spirit. Traditionally, it has represented
passion, creativity, love, and renewal — all of which are
governed by the spirit. Our spirit determines the degree

to which we feel life surging in us, allowing us to generate passion, to "inflame" or inspire others, to renew our enthusiasm for living, and to follow the life path imprinted upon our souls. When we allow our spirit to be centered in our heart, then we live in accordance with the Divine.

Spirit, like fire, can burn out of control or it can flicker so weakly that the slightest wind will extinguish it. Spirit needs air, and soul needs water. Too much soul will douse the fire of spirit, and too much spirit will boil the water of the soul. What it "boils" down to is that too much spirit can bring too much struggle. Too much melting into soul can bring complacency, or a tendency to swallow things whole, so that we define ourselves as "victims" of life with no choice but to accept our tired lot in life.

In other words, too much striving to use our free will to bypass life's lessons, only creates problems. Although we "create" our own destiny by our choices and attitude, there are things we are here to experience. The experiences of the soul are not always charming, and we wonder why we should have to suffer such trials. But in the long run we take from the experience a great truth, and we use this truth to go in a positive direction.

Fire represents new beginnings and regeneration. Your sacred fire, your spirit, is your own unique power of creative self-expression and self-renewal. A flame signifies the eternal. Within you burns an eternal flame, for the spirit and soul transcend the physical body and physical time. Your flame will continue to burn brightly forever, both in the next world and in the memories and contributions to life that you have left behind.

. . . .

PRACTICE IDEA: *Tending the Sacred Flame*

The first houses and domestic spaces were built around a hearth. I love the word *hearth,* because it has the words *heart* and *earth* embedded in it. The heart is the hearth of our sacred flame, and the body is built around our central flame. Here are some ideas for experiencing the deeper qualities of fire and tending our sacred flame:

- Establish a sacred hearth — a fire for life, not for mere survival.
- Dance around a fire, even if it is only a candle.
- Think about the sound of fire burning, the friendly feeling of the fire spirits, as a roaring fire warms you on a cold dark night.

- Think about what smoke symbolizes. Burn some incense. Hold the burning stick in the light from a window and watch how it brings life to the air.
- Consider what it means to stand in the sacred fire, burn off all of the illusions, and step out as a new being.
- Practice being a free spirit willing to dance in the winds of Heaven with love in your heart, and reverence for your soul.

· 32 ·

SACRED SOUND

What we perceive as sound is really
energy and vibration, the displacement or
movement of molecules in the air,
and all the space that surrounds us —
indoors and out — is full of sound,
whether we have the capacity to hear it.

—PEG STREEP, *Altars Made Easy*

ARRY TRUMAN ONCE SAID that listening to good
music made him think of the way things ought to
be, instead of the way they are. In the presence of music,
everything seems just the way it ought to be at that
moment; we gain a taste of Heaven on Earth. Music is
vitally important to our spiritual health. Music can clear
the air, change our mood, take us to faraway places, reveal
mysteries, and allow us a true glimpse into the past.

If we feel blocked emotionally or creatively, we
can often free the energy by listening to, composing, or
performing music. Music also calms the soul; we sing

babies to sleep with lullabies, and quiet restless, angry, or depressed spirits with soothing melodies. Your soul may be crying out for music right now, to bring you back to your center, your source of inner peace. Music and song engages us on a different level of communication than simply talking. I have met so many people who say they cannot sing; this is absurd. Group singing is also not as prevalent in our world today, and that is a terrible loss.

I spoke earlier about a women's Bible study group I used to attend wherein I experienced many wonderful mystical moments. One afternoon in the Bible study, a woman was invited to sing for us. She sang the song "Let There Be Peace on Earth," a cappella, with pitch so perfect I cannot imagine an angel could sing it better. She happened to be blind and always seemed to be smiling, and while she sang her face radiated divine beauty. The words of the song speak of divine truth, and this woman's singing opened everyone's heart. Soon we were all weeping.

Mary Beth Crain and I wrote in the *Angel Journey Cards*: "Music is also inexorably linked to prayer. Every religion and spiritual tradition has its hymns and songs of praise to God. The angels are invariably depicted as singing praises to the glory of God in vast celestial choirs, or as playing harps and lyres. The widely held belief in the congruence between the seven notes of the musical scale, the seven spectral colors, and the seven chakras or energy fields that surround the body may explain why chanting, for instance, is such a powerful form of prayer. The monks of the Tibetan Tantric Choir perform concerts all over the world, in which they chant for world peace. Chanting is an expression of joy and reverence that elevates our vibrations, expanding our connection to all of humanity and, eventually, the entire universe."

The other night I was watching a television show about a couple of scientists who developed a telescope that could take measurements throughout the Universe. They found the same sound or pattern of radiation occurring everywhere they took a measurement, and one physicist described this as the "music of the spheres," the "cosmic chant" that Pythagoras spoke of in 500 B.C. The theories connected to this sound bring forth the idea that all cells have a vibration, like a vibrating string within. There is a divine beat of the Universe; when we tune into it, when it seems as if our heart is beating with the divine pulse, then we feel centered and at home in our being.

One of my concerns about digital music is the sterilization of the sound. I just don't feel it is right, and I often get a slight headache from listening to compact disks for too long. Give me back someone's cough or the keys dropping in the background; I want the whole musical experience, not a digitized simulation of it. Forcing things into perfection often leaves no room for spirit. The human touch is what carries the energy and opens our hearts.

We can think of ourselves as musical instruments that imprint the world in a unique way. Our body is the instrument, our nerves are the strings, and the musician is our spirit. When you're in a music store and you pluck a string on a guitar, all the other guitars in the room will vibrate to that tone. We are like these guitars, vibrating to a heavenly tone. What type of music are you making? The angels would like to see us use our instruments to develop a harmonious blending of soul, spirit, temple, and mind. As Manly P. Hall has said, "Beauty is harmony manifesting its own intrinsic nature in the world of form."

We have a divine instinct for harmony. Discordance can be interesting and useful in expressions of art and music, but harmony is divine because it manifests beauty. Beauty nourishes us on many levels; it has incredible tranformational power. Harmony is the manifesting expression of the will of God. Goodness, in order to carry the divine vibration, must act in accordance with its own nature, which creates harmony. The angels are often depicted as singing praises to God all day; they are gathered into groups defined as choirs. This image in art can be found throughout history. We can listen for the angels singing along with choirs; we do have the ears to hear.

. . . .

PRACTICE IDEA: *Musical Harmony*

Pay attention to harmony in your world. Where do you find it, where is it lacking, and how does it manifest within you? Music has been found to help plants to grow and to heal disease. If you are experiencing illness or a wilting of energy in any way, explore the healing power of music. What type of music do you crave when you feel agitated? Listen to your favorite music; move with it. Take up an instrument or start a dance class. Do whatever is necessary to bring vitality and physical balance back into your life.

Save up some money, and if one of your favorite musical groups is in town giving a concert, go experience them in person. I urge you to listen to live music whenever you can. When you listen to classical music performed live, let your imagination take you on a journey;

it will restore your being like nothing else. If the chemistry is conducive, you will hear the angels sing.

If you are interested in an in-depth study of sound and its divine effect on us, read *Sacred Sounds: Transformation Through Music and Word* by Ted Andrews.

· 33 ·

THE ART AND PRACTICE
OF "ECCENTERING"

The one quality that seems to be universal among
eccentrics is not on our list, because it is so subjective
as to be incapable of being proved or disproved, yet it
may be the most important: eccentrics appear to be
happier than the rest of us . . . nearly everyone we
met seemed to be pretty contented with his lot in life.
Almost all of them exuded a sense of being comfortable
with who they were. They were aware of the fact that many
people found them strange, but it didn't bother them.
—DR. DAVID WEEKS AND JAMIE JAMES, *Eccentrics*

THE WORD ECCENTRIC COMES from the Greek word *ekkentros,* which means *not* having the same center. These days, not having the same center as the "world" is a saving grace. Having our own center is what we need to stay sane in a world that seems to be hanging by millions of fraying threads. In order to thrive, we must have a strong center that we know how to get back to under any circumstance. Restrained perfection and well-adjusted behavior doesn't mean we are centered inside. We all need to have a divine shelter within, to protect our divine qualities.

I am using the term *eccentering* to represent the art of living as a free spirit. Eccentering ourselves is a means for finding ways to be happy in being who we are, to get back to what is real, to not be afraid of what is known but not seen (such as the angels), and to have courage to expand our notion of reality.

The following questions are based on my idea of what denotes eccentric traits, and are partly based on the criteria, profile, and characteristics noticed by the authors of the book *Eccentrics: A Study of Sanity and Strangeness,* Dr. David Weeks and Jamie James.

- Do you have a mischievous sense of humor?
- Are you noncompetitive and happy to be this way?
- Do you, in the opinion of others or yourself, have unusual eating habits and living arrangements?
- Are you able to not "live down" to others' expectations, or be influenced by their opinions of you?
- Do you have a different sense of what time it is?
- Is daydreaming an important activity for you?
- Do you have any hobbies that have taken you places others have not dared to go?
- Are you strongly motivated by curiosity?

- Do you feel you have a higher calling in life, but that it is not necessarily something you need a literal mission statement for?
- Do you want the world to be a happier place with more eccentrics enjoying themselves?
- Do you naturally listen to people?
- Can you talk freely to animals and plants?
- Have you ever been labeled intelligent?
- Are you comfortable in being creative, by your own standards?
- Have you ever heard the words *nonconformist, unconventional, weird, strange,* or *odd* used in reference to you?
- Did you hear them as a child?
- Do you feel like you are in step with the "real world," and the rest of the world is operating out of step?
- Do you question collective assumptions and general sentimental thinking most people fall right into?
- Do you often feel you have been let in on a private cosmic joke that others have missed?

If you answered yes to at least three of the above questions, then you have an eccentric nature, and the angels want to help you enjoy it by offering you a way to be happy just being who you are. People who are on a quest for perfection will never be able to relax into themselves; eccentered people can always do this and it drives others crazy. Humans who are more awake and eccentric face special challenges because the consensus reality is so different from the way they see and experience life. Sadly, society may even drive them crazy if they don't have a strong spiritual center or sense of themselves.

When we find our own center, strengthen it by our own spiritual practices, and then enjoy ourselves, we *will* be happier. In other words, we all have the capacity in some small way to be eccentric, and that is why we need to "eccenter" ourselves — to find our sacred center and keep it strong. The best thing about eccentering ourselves is that it is creative, satisfying, meaningful, and something the angels can take direct part in.

Some of the most blessed gifts the angels offer are ways to bring us back to our own center, regardless of the situation. To be centered means to feel that our soul, spirit, body, and mind are harmoniously working together, happily basking in the warmth of inner peace. There are many assaults on our centeredness in today's world, and the angels can help us to understand and counteract the uncentering forces. You can find your own sacred center, but remember you are not alone; the angels love to help with this special quest. Your center is only a prayer away.

. . . .

PRACTICE IDEA: *Eccentering Yourself*

Sometimes we have trouble staying centered. Our soul seems stuck outside us somewhere, our spirit is uninspired, our body feels foreign to us, and our mind has taken over with worries and concerns.

If you are sensing a quickening at this time on the planet, it doesn't mean you need to speed up your life or jump on the fast track. All that is needed is to find the center of your being and spend some time there every day. We are on a planet that is spinning in space, yet we don't feel dizzy from the spinning because we are right here, right now, in bodies designed to be part of life on Earth. If you are experiencing too much chaos and confusion, it is a signal that you need to get back to the present and eccenter yourself. If you have to live your life labeled as an eccentric in order to be true to yourself, then enter fully into it and have some fun.

34

CIVILIZED
REVERENCE

Watch your thoughts; they become words.
Watch your words; they become actions.
Watch your actions; they become habits.
Watch your habits; they become your character.
Watch your character; it becomes your destiny.

—FRANK OUTLAW

IF WE COULD DISTILL the basic message of the angels, of Jesus, and of Buddha, I think we would find that spiritually minded and heart-centered compassionate reverence is the essence of each. Reverence allows us to connect deeply with the essence of life, so that we are able to respect the Buddha nature in all things. Our birth represents an agreement we made to experience the physical reality of passion, pain, love, and greatness that humans are capable of. But most of all the agreement we made included the commitment to practice reverence, which is to honor the sacred life. When I think of the world today,

I can't help but believe that pure compassion energized by the streams of light from Heaven would heal so many situations that seem wrong and evil.

Reverence is the quality that makes humans compassionate. True reverence is not annulled when we are angry, or facing other difficult emotions. Too often humans fall into attack mode when they are angry and unhappy. Instead, when we revere life, our anger and sadness will not allow us to hurt another form of life. We must remember that other people are not here to make us happy or unhappy, nor are they to blame for anything we are going through. We are here, as the writer Manly P. Hall said, "to cooperate and cheat the devil."

Lack of reverence on any level of life creates a painful imbalance in the world's soul. Where reverence is present and counted for, love is given back to life, and balance is restored. When we get to the point where our perceptions are shaped by reverence, we will realize that to become a helpless victim in life is one of the least reverent things we can do. We have to have reverence for ourselves in order to have reverence for life. That is why it is so important to acknowledge what is reverent and what is not.

Over the years I have always enjoyed the work of the ever-interesting and entertaining Buddhist scholar Robert Thurman. Recently I came upon his comments on civilization and found them to contain an angelic message. He discusses civilization as a complex of human qualities that have enabled a wide variety of people to live in cities together. He uses the Tibetans as a model of the last traces of real civilized living. Thurman found that the qualities of civilized behavior, as understood by various sociologists and himself, fall into four main categories:

1. *Individualism:* Free from collectively imposed roles and identities and able to be a unique person in interactions with others.
2. *Flexibility of character:* Sensitivity to others, and the ability to adapt personality to various roles, enabling people to adapt . . . to pluralistic situations of a city.
3. *Gentleness:* The ability to restrain violent impulses and pursue success and resolution of conflict in nonviolent ways, which makes individualism and flexibility possible.
4. *Contentment and creativity:* The ability to enjoy life, pursue happiness, and seek satisfaction in imaginative, original, and nontraditional ways.

I find it interesting to think about a civilized way of life, mostly because I have been hearing the word *barbaric* quite a bit lately in reference to certain current events. The traits that embody barbarism, in contrast are:

1. Tribalism, racism, fanaticism, nationalism.
2. Rigidity, selfish insistence on one's own perspective.
3. Wrathfulness and addiction to violence.
4. Fixation on routine misery, unhappiness, and accepting misery, which leads to obsession with wealth, status, power, and competitiveness, and to prejudice, exclusiveness, violence, insatiable greed, fragmentation of community, overpopulation, pollution, and other social ills.

Civilized reverence means we must look honestly and compassionately at what is going on in our own psyche and the psyche of the world — in our body and the body of the earth; in our heart and the heart of the world; in our spirit and the spirit of the times we live in; in our soul and in the *animus mundi,* the soul of the world.

. . . .

PRACTICE IDEA: *Reverence*

If you truly want to know the angels, then start with a simple intention of being more reverent. To cultivate this quality, you don't need your guardian angel's name, you don't need to see an angel, and you don't need direct verbal guidance. All you need is love in your heart and the courage to let it shine as healing light. The angels need you as much as you need them. Instead of focusing on the supernatural qualities of angels, focus on the angelic qualities within you. You have the choice to be compassionate and civilized, or selfish and barbaric. It is up to you. Dedicate one day this week to practicing reverence.

35

ANGELIC
INSIGHTS

If human beings knew that beautiful, good,
and powerful beings were watching us,
maybe we would stand up more erect
and be more beautiful ourselves.
We would be inspired to live up to our dignity.

—MATTHEW FOX

IN THIS CHAPTER, I present some of the insights and perceptions I have come across over the years regarding angels and how they interact with us. All of these ideas about angels strike a knowing feeling in my heart.

- The angels vibrate at such a refined frequency that when they want us to receive a message, they know how to get it through quick.
- If the angels need to visit us and change our direction in life, they can alter our perception so that when they leave, the change stays, but our experience of the "angel"

is hidden in our unconscious like the contents of an out-of-reach dream.

- I have never doubted people when they were telling me about an experience they have had with the angels. Regardless of what level of sensation they relay, it is not up to me to doubt the experience they had that deeply affected them.
- The angels have a delightful sense of humor.
- The angels help us to evolve and to love. If your own special way of evolving spells success in the eyes of the world, so be it, but don't get too caught up in it. The world is not the source of love; God is the source of love.
- The angels are present to remind us that our problems may prove to be our salvation, as we learn to replace self-recrimination with self-love, shame with awareness, judgment with observation, and fear with freedom of spirit.
- Angels live in the eternal realm; our sense of time doesn't limit them.
- Essential qualities such as hope, love, gratitude, reverence, and an open heart allow us a strong ongoing connection with the angels.
- The angels do not belong to a particular religion. Believe it or not, in this "enlightened society" of ours, some people still claim that angels are affiliated with only one religion, or one type of person. The angels are

available to everyone, because each human carries the light of Heaven in his or her heart, and the angels work for Heaven.

• Light attracts light. The angels are attracted to our light, and exist to help us shine brighter.

• Angel consciousness is knowing you are a divine being, and that you are guided by a higher wisdom in the Universe that operates for your highest good.

• Angel consciousness points us to the fact that life is meant to be enjoyed and lived, not suffered and endured.

• In the realm of the angels, thoughts are the same as actions. The thoughts you hold in your mind at any given moment are like forms to the angels. This is good news because the angels have direct access to your thoughts if you want them to, and can help direct your thoughts to a higher spiritual level.

• Our guardian angels are connected with our survival. They are with us all the time and can do amazing things when our lives are threatened as long as our instinct for survival is positive and thriving. The guardian angels of those humans who have a death wish and really want to destroy themselves have to step back because they cannot participate in this desire and can only take action if the life-affirming force comes back and the humans change their mind and ask for help.

- One way our guardian angel protects us is by keeping our brain positively programmed to be life affirming and to build self-esteem. The angels have a constant battle with this task because our minds are influenced so easily and too often we hear messages that work against the positive.

- One of the gifts from the angels is that regardless of how dark it seems at times, or how hard life seems to be getting, a spark of hope begins to grow, and when we are ready it lights up our life and things are different. The good things in life are always with us; we just need to position ourselves to notice them.

- Angels are important to us for many reasons, which are difficult to intellectualize; it is a matter of heart and humor — getting us to think on our own and lighten up.

- When we become aware of the love and guidance always available from the angels, a big change occurs in our life due to an angelic uplifting of our consciousness. Something actually changes in us, and we feel new impulses.

- Sometimes angels are walking with you and seen by others who may want to harm you, yet you do not see them, or even realize they are near.

- When you walk into a store and a song about angels is playing, it makes you feel better instantly. Walk into this store a week later, and you may find that yet another song about angels is playing. The angels are creative in the ways they remind us of their presence; we need to pay creative attention.

- The angels are like the little playmates who came to your house when you were young and stood outside waiting for you to notice them so you would want to come out and play. The angels are not known to knock on the door and give you orders to come out and play; they want you to notice them and freely choose to join them.

- An angel can appear in human form and can save you from anything according to divine will. If they need to stop a train or throw you out of harm's way, they are capable of doing this. If it is your time for rebirth on the other side, they will go with you, but they cannot prevent your death if it is divine will; that is between you and the Creator.

- Watch the sky and remember to notice what is above you. Look up often, and also notice what is below you. Too often we just notice what is at eye level and miss out on things above, below, and behind us.

- Pay attention to "God in the details," and you will find angels.

- There are many kinds of angels — guardian angels, muses, angels of the inner psyche, ancestor angels, nature guardians, angels of the moment, happiness trainers, angels of the divine feminine energy, and overlighting angels of countries, groups, relationships, and so forth. We can learn to have a give-and-take relationship with the many faces of angels.

- Our relationship with the angels will grow strong if we treat it as a sacred relationship. We don't have to fully understand all the particulars. When it is time to go deeper, we will find little ways to delight the angels daily, with our creative energy and by bringing beauty into our homes through flowers, art, and so on. We can share things with them, and they will broadcast the love and beauty through the ethers for those who have the eyes to behold and the ears to hark.

- Angels are symbolic of our divine connection to the ultimate Source of Love. Symbols and images reach us on a deep level and allow us to recognize energy fields, such as the angels.

- The angels are here to lead us to our higher self and to God, and at the same time to allow us to honor the experience of being human, not dismiss the physical.

- The angels never ask us to become angels or pure spirit, but to become more angelic in our ways. To become more angelic gives us a deeper wisdom we didn't think we had the capacity for, and allows us to look at ourselves from a divine and noble perspective.

. . . .

PRACTICE IDEA: *Enlightenment*

The five integral facets of "en-lighten-ment" are love, gratitude, wisdom, humility, and compassion, which lead to humor, grace, intelligence, caring, and reverence. Here are some thoughts that may help you to develop these qualities and stay connected to the angels:

- Pay attention to "the little things" in life, the special gifts the angels give us in our daily life that we often miss unless we pause with a moment of gratitude.
- Think about how you can put new spirit and soul into your relationship with God and the angels.
- Have you expected the angels to perform worldly tasks that may not support your highest good? If so, did this leave you with a lack of faith when the angels didn't help with things outside their dominion?
- Think about real ways you have changed since receiving your expanded view of the angels. Are you more aware now? Are you beginning to see the world without the net of your beliefs cast over it?

• Pay attention, and if possible, note in writing anytime you think about the angels, ask the angels for insight, and feel peace in knowing they are with you.

Following is a list of qualities that people mention when I ask them which qualities of angel consciousness help them connect, understand, experience, and love the angels. Select the qualities that you wish to cultivate and then ask the angels to help you.

Abundance
Beauty
Charity
Clarity
Comfort
Compassion
Courage
Divine harmony
Enthusiasm
Faith
Flexibility
Forgiveness
Freedom
Generosity
Gentleness

Grace and gracefulness
Gratitude
Harmony
Hope
Humility
Humor
Joy
Light
Love
Might
Original innocence
Pain
Passion
Patience
Peace
Play
Reflection
Release
Reverence
Simplicity
Strength
Understanding
Wisdom
Wonder

Gratitude and love, two qualities of the heart, help all the other qualities to flourish in our beings. I wish you all these angelic qualities and many blessings as you continue your journey along the path of angel consciousness.

"The angel who presided o'er my birth said, 'Little creature formed of joy and mirth, go and love without the help of anything on earth.'"
—WILLIAM BLAKE

ACKNOWLEDGMENTS

"No one is a failure who has friends," as Clarence the angel told George Bailey in the movie *It's a Wonderful Life*. I had one of those *It's a Wonderful Life* years, when you feel as if you have been cast out from everything familiar and secure, when things fall away like dust in a windstorm, and when you truly learn who your real friends are. I don't know how I got so lucky in the friend department, but my life is wonderful in infinite ways because of the incredible people I can call friends.

I wrote my first book ten years ago, in 1988, and was blessed to work with Uma Reed and Nancy Carleton. We have reunited once again on this book, in a new home: Amber-Allen Publishing. Uma is beauty manifested in a multitude of ways, and I thank her for being there for me with her friendship during the orbit of this book. It is such a blessing and comfort to know that Nancy Carleton will be the editor when I am writing a book. She emanates strength, gentleness, and wisdom; what more could you ask for in a friend and editor? Janet Mills, publisher at Amber-Allen, let me know right away that her raison d'être is to create a *home,* rather than a publishing house, for creative vision. Believe me, in the publishing world it is rare to find this, and I feel very blessed that Janet took an interest in this book. It has been a pleasure to get to know her this year.

Loretta Barrett, my agent, really pulled through and let me know she believed in me above and beyond the rise and fall of angel book popularity. She is a remarkable woman, and I am so blessed to have her in my life as a friend and mediator to the world out there.

My special love, Joe Kelly Jackson, truly supported me in many ways during the writing of this book. I am forever grateful to him and his strong, warm character.

Shannon Melikan has been with me through much of the past twenty-four years. We have found ourselves in so many different "worlds" together, and she has been a friend beyond what anyone could ask for and a true soul sister. Once again, I thank her for her humor, love, gracefulness, and sharing the vision of angel consciousness.

Holly Phillips and I have known each other since age seven. After years of parallel journeying, the angels brought us back together in 1994. What a blessing to have a friend like Holly; I thank her for sharing her spirit of fun and delight with me when I felt lost this past year.

I met Mary Beth Crain-Shields ten years ago when I first had the notion to write *Messengers of Light*. We have shared so much together: writing, playing, facing hardship, and most important, laughing after all is said and done. I thank her for bringing so much richness into my life.

Sister Janet Harris brought a new dimension of light, inspiration, and friendship into my life this year. She is the founder and guardian angel of the Inside/Out writing program at Central Juvenile Hall in Los Angeles, and brought me in as a writing facilitator. I never experienced this level of the true transformative power of writing and expression until joining this program. I thank Sister Janet, and I thank the writers I have met, young men who are facing a tough destiny and already have more character and knowledge about what it means to be a man than many forty-year-olds I know.

I thank my family for the unconditional love and support that has always been available to me. I know I have been quite a challenge to raise and send out into the world, because I do hear a different drummer in the distance and have stubbornly insisted on tracking down the music I hear out there in the mystery. This has never been easy for those who love me, and I'm truly grateful for their presence in my life.

I wish to thank many courageous friends committed to keeping angel consciousness alive, all in their unique and blessed ways:

Jai Italiaander (see dedication), of Angels on Call, destiny consultant and intuitive reader.

K. Martin-Kuri, author of *Message for the Millennium* and guiding light behind The New Millennium Sanctuary for Love, Wisdom, and Grace in Virginia, a sacred community forming on sacred land.

Arthur Douët, artist and teacher. His paintings give people a glimpse of the angels' world and help us remember whence we came. Just thinking about Arthur makes me smile!

Kirk and Sandy Moore of Tara's Angels, a beautiful store in San Juan Capistrano, California. Kirk is author of *Tara's Angels,* a special book in which he shares his story of spiritual healing after great loss.

Allan Duncan of Angels Without Wings. He is always up to something beautiful and interesting, and is responsible for inspiring many people of all ages to use their own courage to greet life.

Don and Lucy at Wings of Freedom retreat center, nestled in a sacred spot in the mountains of Ojai, California.

Peter Sterling with his Harp Magic and dedication to creating a healing experience of the angels when he plays his harp.

My long-time close friends Laurel and Larry Savoie of universalmind.com and creators of "Children of the Sun." I thank them for being there for me many times during the past year with their humor, love, wise counsel, and experience in relationship. They are great friends and fellow keepers of the dream.

I thank all the *Angels Can Fly* members who have been so sweet and supportive over the years.

I thank God — and of course, the angels.

—Terry Lynn Taylor, May 1998

A Note from the Author

I have written several books concerning angel consciousness, and the focus of each one corresponded with what I felt to be an important aspect of the infinite consciousness. My first book, *Messengers of Light,* I wrote in response to what I was experiencing. It was scary in a way because even though I knew others were also having a deeper experience with the angels, I felt that I didn't have any teachers to follow except the angels themselves. I had the insight to invite readers to write to me so I could start a newsletter. From the letters, I got a sense that people were interested in how the angels help us help ourselves, so I wrote *Guardians of Hope* and included many self-help practices and ideas about how Heaven helps us. After that book, I wanted to share some of the letters I had received, so I put together *Answers from the Angels.*

I found I loved the way people, inspired by the angels, were expressing their creativity in honor of the Divine. When I was giving talks and workshops, people would share with me how they had made radical changes in their lives in order to do more meaningful and creative work — even if it meant less money and a much simpler existence. So I wrote *Creating with the Angels* to help spur the momentum on.

Keeping a journal or diary is one important way I've found for staying somewhat sane. I started doing this when I was about ten. *Messengers of Light* was first conceived in my journal writings. By writing about my feelings and thoughts about angels, I was able to have "visible proof" that my consciousness was changing in a very welcome way. I always wanted a journal that would offer inspiration and give me a place to write down my goals, prayer requests, the angels I am calling on, and the things that are worrying me. I designed *Angel Days* to include all of this as well as a little space to write each day. When we keep track of our spiritual growth, even in little ways, we see how miraculous life really is.

Angels Can Fly Newsletter is a quarterly reminder to keep the angels in your heart, published by Terry Lynn Taylor. You can order tapes and other books by T. L. T. through the newsletter.

The membership fee is $13.00 (or gratis if you can't afford the fee at this time). For a sample copy of *Angels Can Fly,* send a self-addressed-stamped-envelope (#10 business size) to:

Terry Lynn Taylor
2275 Huntington Drive, #326
San Marino, CA 91108

Please feel free to write about your own angel experiences, feelings, questions, or whatever is on your mind. Write if you want information on good sources for music, readings, and anything else that will help you keep your angel consciousness alive and well.

It is time to join together as a unique angel network, to help the angels and in turn help humanity.

Amber-Allen Publishing is dedicated to bringing
a message of love and inspiration to all who seek
a higher purpose and meaning in life.

For a free catalog of our books and cassettes,
please contact:

Amber-Allen Publishing
Post Office Box 6657
San Rafael, California 94903

(800) 624-8855 (phone)
(415) 499-3174 (fax)

Email: amberallen@infoasis.com
Visit our website: http://www.amberallen.com